The OTHER Evangelism

*One Man's View
of Evangelism in Depth's
Revolutionary Results*

by Juan M. Isais

Translated into English by Elisabeth F. Isais

Privada de Agustin Gutierrez 67,
03340 Mexico, D.F., Mexico
Tel. 688-2948

July 1988

Dedication

Dedicated to my wife, Elisabeth, with all my heart; without her help this book would not have been possible; and to my four children, Raquel, Cynthia, Sally, and Juan David, who paid a high price for having their father involved in Evangelism in Depth but who today are all actively participating in the service of the Lord.

Contents

Foreword

The author of this book, a humble, gentle and loving servant of God, has had a profound effect on my own personal life and ministry. When I first met him, laboring in a remote village north of Mexico City in 1987, I thought of the words of John the Baptist: "He must increase, but I must decrease" (John 3:30 NKJV). Juan Isais is the founder and director of the Latin America Mission of Mexico, known as MILAMEX. As an evangelist, he has preached in numerous countries throughout the world. He was associate evangelist with Billy Graham in the Caribbean Crusade in 1958, and served as an instructor at Amsterdam '86. He and his wife, Elisabeth, have produced such notable works as *The Other Side of the Coin, Evangelism in Depth,* and *The Other Revolution.* He has been a composer of gospel songs and choruses that Christians have sung around the world. Yet, despite such noteriety, Juan has enjoyed a strange sort of anonymity, becoming almost a victim, as it were, of his own philosophy. This will become evident as one studies this work. Rather than giving readers another how-to-do it manual, written from the viewpoint of an "expert," Juan directs his message to the multitudes of believers who **desire** to evangelize, but find themselves paralyzed with fear and the resultant guilt because they have **not** done it. The "how-to" in this case has been left to the creativity of the Holy Spirit within each individual Christian. *The Other Evangelism* is the culmination of the author's observations, insight, and understanding of what the Scriptures say about sharing one's faith, matured in the crucible of his unique personal experience.

What Juan Isais has spearheaded in many parts of the Third World has been historically known as Evangelism in Depth, and that is the term used throughout this book. However, Juan's burden is to see believers mobilized for evangelism in the United States as well. It has been my privilege to hear him share these principles and illustrations on a number of occasions in witnessing seminars conducted in various congregations of the Fellowship of Grace Brethren Churches. Based on this foundation, we have developed our own conception of things and named our program, First Love Renewal, patterning it after the rebuke of our Lord to the church at Ephesus: "Yet, I hold this against you: You have

forsaken your first love" (Revelation 2:4). Our experiments with First
Love Renewals began in 1987, but they have actually been the culmination of 20 years of prayer by the author of this book. I have listened
to Juan Isais tearfully and sincerely confess his own willingness to die
for America, if need be, to see Christians within these shores mobilized
into a mighty, conqueroring army for our Saviour. It is our sincere prayer
that God, by His Holy Spirit, will use this little volume to remove the
guilt and fear believers hold because they have not shared their faith;
may it spark a revival within the Body of Christ, and stir the hearts of
God's children back to their first love!

> Ron E. Thompson, Executive Director
> Brethren Evangelistic Ministries

Preface

Like everyone else, I love to ask questions. For many years I have sought answers to many of them which on the surface may seem simple, but their depth sometimes threatens to drown me. For example:

Why do churches shunt evangelism to one side?

Why is it that when an evangelism course is given in a church, regardless of which organization gives it, a good group of people starts out practicing the ideas but before long, only a very small number continues?

Why is it that countries which are always exporting evangelistic technology have no solution for their own problems, and if their churches grow it is at the expense of other denominations?

Why do new students arrive at our theological seminaries full of faith, fervor, and evangelistic zeal, but when they finally go out into the pastorate they seem to have lost their faith and their passion to win souls?

Why do the false sects that only teach part of the truth seem to grow so much in comparison with true Christianity?

Why do our people deny themselves the privilege of sharing their faith with others even when they are constantly exhorted to witness?

Why have so many religious leaders abandoned personal evangelism and even question it?

Why do the denominations continue to use the same methods and strategies even though they see they are losing people, or in the best of circumstances they are not growing?

Why do the experts give solutions to the problems of others regarding evangelism, but do not solve their own?

Why do the denominations have such tiny budgets for evangelism when it ought to be the number one reason for the church's existence?

Why have we abandoned Christ's strategies and methods and substituted our own?

In the following pages I hope the reader may find some light in regard to these questions. The answers will be as varied as our concepts and definitions of evangelism, but no one who reads with an open mind, without prejudices or pretensions outside of the Bible, can keep going in the same defeatist way in evangelism.

At least that it is my hope.

Introduction

Evangelism and evangelizing have been my constant passion since I came to know Christ as Saviour. As a matter of fact, all my Christian life and ministerial career has been dedicated to promoting cooperative evangelism.

When I was a very new believer, attending the Presbyterian church, someone taught me that Pentecostals worshipped Satan. My curiosity led me to visit one of their services in the church pastored at the time by the Rev. Arnulfo Espinoza on August 28th street in a section of Mexico City known as Tacubaya.

There I heard things that gave rise to many questions which I shared with my pastor, who then went with me to a service and concluded that these people were indeed our brothers and sisters in Christ.

"They believe the same as we do," he advised me, "but they have a different style of practicing their faith."

That experience opened my eyes and I began to understand that the Church is something more than a denominational concept. My pastor taught me to love other Christians, to work with them in evangelism, and to look for the good side of each group. Today I clearly understand that all Christ-centered and Bible believing groups are part of His Body.

Years have gone by and my experiences have not always been easy. Paraphrasing the apostle Paul, I can say to the Latin American evangelical world, "You yourselves know how I did not shrink from declaring to you anything that was profitable, teaching you with prayer and many tears so that you could unite in the great and exciting task of proclaiming the Gospel, presenting a united image and effort."

The Lord has given me practice in this area and therefore many people have suggested I write. The truth is that I have been afraid to try to express what I have taught for so many years. I fear someone will confuse what I write with some kind of a program, so that Evangelism in Depth will become mechanized and then die. Nevertheless, more than ever I have come to the conclusion that in the end what is written is what endures.

So with the help of God, and my wife who continually inspires me and has written about Evangelism in Depth ever since the beginning in

1960, I have tried to share here the idea that has dominated my evangelistic task. That is, that God gives us the ability to handle eternal truths adequately from the very moment of our conversion, adjusted to the needs of the listener; and also that Christians lose their natural ability to evangelize in direct relationship to the methods they are taught in order to do it.

I have never stopped believing and practicing that there are as many evangelistic methods as there are people who need the Gospel and opportunities to share it. This is what has maintained evangelistic fervor in my life and is what I wish to share with you.

This book is organized in such a way that I hope you will find in it the motivation to evangelize, but also the price that must be paid to do it. To love all the brethren is not always easy, because with all the love we preach about, it is not common to work together. But evangelism, God's number one love, demands the exercise of that Christian love which necessarily goes beyond the favorite doctrines of each member of the Body of Christ. In any case, the dominant note must be that we are united so the world may believe.

There is no doubt that each believer is the center of his or her own social universe and to reach that group, he or she requires nothing more than obedience. But the need of giving a united witness is a tool that in the final analysis principally benefits those who do it.

To evangelize with the criteria and methods Christ Himself used, is the only answer for the fulfillment of the Great Commission. The concept of addition which dominates the major part of our evangelistic activities, continues to give results, but only feeble ones compared with those obtainable when the theology of evangelism changes from the pulpit to the individual.

This formula, and only this, is our hope for accelerating the second coming of Christ, because the Scripture teaches that He will not return until the Church is complete. Let us not forget that "the Lord is not slow in keeping his promise, as some understand slowness. He is patient with you, not wanting anyone to perish, but everyone to come to repentance" (II Peter 3:9).

Intentionally, in different contexts I have repeated the fundamental concepts that have made Evangelism in Depth a romantic and passionately exciting task wherever its ideas have been taught, since its principal characteristic is that the believer goes back to his first love.

In the heart of this book you will find the methods of Christ, without any commentary. That is why these ideas are irresistible.

And one more word. The thesis presented here does not promote improvisation in any way, shape or form in order to grow in the Christian life. What it does promote, is that the qualitative and quantitative growth of the church is in direct relationship to the success which can be obtained in teaching the ordinary believer that when it comes to evangelism, he is more effective than the professional communicator in the moment when he is willing to do it. For this reason the church grew by the thousands in the first century.

Chapter 1

Miss Paulson and Other Important People

Let me tell you about three great people who affected my life and ministry.

I met Kenneth Strachan through an extraordinary evangelist who unfortunately abandoned the ministry later on. To that eloquent preacher I owe the fact that I knew one of the outstanding Christian statesmen of his time: Kenneth Strachan, man of vision, impassioned in everything he did. And because of that, I was permitted the services of one of his teams to help me shake up the world in which I moved at the time.

I was dedicated to mobilizing young people when we became acquainted, and he was nothing but an inspiration in my life.

I also knew Miss Eleanor Paulson, a missionary with uncommon knowledge and sense of responsibility. She was my missions teacher. I still recall how she gave of herself in class and how her fervent lessons made our hearts beat faster and inflamed us with the desire to go out and conquer the world for Christ, even though it meant dying for the cause.

Not a single class went by during which I did not weep for the lost. Those tears and the concepts she poured into us have followed me through the years, and as has been said of others, I say of her: She was a woman who ran on her knees and knew how to share her ideas successfully.

I knew Pastor Israel Gutierrez Ovando, in some ways a simple man but very wise, a young pastor then with an uncommon ability to identify with others. It was in his church where I was "officially" converted to Christ, because I had heard the Gospel previously and on one occasion at a movie I was moved by these words:

"What shall it profit a man, if he gain the whole world but loses his soul?"

This text jolted my very being and transformed my life.

Pastor Gutierrez put up with me in the early days of my Christian infancy. And he allowed me to introduce a song into the church which roughly translated from Spanish goes like this:

"Only the power of God can make you new;
The proof is that He has transformed me.
Do you see that I am happy serving the Lord?
I am a new creature; I am new!"

I'm not sure where I learned it, but I taught it so much that to this day some people think I was the composer, even though the hymnals publish it as by an unknown author.

Israel, as we young people referred to our pastor, is still alive. He gave me confidence, fear of God, and a sense of urgency for the cause of the Lord. Precisely when I began my new Christian life, I had the privilege of suffering together with him for the Kingdom.

At the time we were in Mexico City, in Lira Park. I can still remember and emotionally feel that old shoe full of stones that hit me on my right cheek while we were holding an open air meeting. Every Sunday we took to the streets and parks to seek the lost. Our pastor organized us so that part of the group, including me, was assigned to protect the girls; others sang, distributed tracts, and invited people to a brief meeting during which they testified about what God had done for them.

One day Israel approached me and said, "It's your turn."

"Mine? What should I say?"

"What God has done for you."

What an unforgettable day! I trembled and perspired, but when I finished a few young people responded and went with us to the church.

From my pastor I learned many ideas about total mobilization, although he never used that name. By the way, from that youth group in a very short time more than 30 of us, a very high percentage, dedicated our lives to serve the Lord full-time.

I also knew a composer, preacher, and musician, Alfredo Colom. He was the spark that made me begin to reflect seriously about evangelizing this way. He was the invited preacher, I was the songleader, and there were others on the team. During the 50's Colom was one of the best evangelists, powerful in the word and in deeds. When he preached people wept and came forward, willing to pay the price of following the Lord. His message was simple but full of power. His style was unconventional.

Through his music, with Gospel words for Latin rhythms, he prepared the hearts of his non-Christian hearers as well as cold backslidden believers. One of his popular tunes goes like this:

"Why should I sin, if I am saved, if I have this much light?
Why should I sin, if God has given me life in Jesus?
Why should I sin, if the sinner's only hope is hell?
Why should I sin, why sin against God?

Better to live in holiness, victorious against evil,
Since Jesus is preparing an eternal home for His saints,
A beautiful land in the heavens
Where the unclean may not go in.
Why should I sin, why sin, why sin against God?''

Every night multitudes arrived at the campaign anxious to hear the message of the Lord. Colom was so full of zeal to share his convictions that once he removed his jacket right on the platform and threw it to the floor, illustrating a point in his sermon. His message was simple, I repeat, but very powerful.

Nevertheless, one day in our morning session with the local committee, the leaders asked Kenneth Strachan to remove Colom from the campaign and send another preacher who would be more elevated in style and more acceptable to the leaders. And Don Kenneth, as we called Dr. Strachan, agreed to send him elsewhere.

Incidents such as this, some even more shameful, brought anguish to my soul and led me to think that this concentric model of evangelism could be substituted for something better, or that perhaps there might be alternatives with less risk, although at the time I probably did not comprehend everything that was deep in my mind nor in Dr. Strachan's.

But a serious reflective process regarding evangelization had begun in me, even though I was a member of the coordinating group of the campaign department of the Latin America Mission with headquarters in San Jose, Costa Rica.

Don Kenneth frequently invited me to chat about these problems and about the evangelistic work we were carrying out. There I realized that our long-term planning did produce some results, but less than what we hoped for, because as soon as we would leave the country where we held the campaigns, the Christians would seem to lose the dimensions of enthusiasm, faith, and dynamics which the task requires.

Dr. Strachan, great friend and to a certain extent my protector and mentor, constantly worried about results. At times he and I spent entire days talking and considering what was happening around us. For me, being young and inexperienced, it was a great privilege.

Chapter 2

Calle Blancos: Seeds of Revolution

Time passed and due to Dr. Strachan's deception with traditional evangelistic campaigns, or perhaps because my predecessor (The Rev. William Thompson) was getting tired, the activity with campaigns began to change and so I was invited to work in radio. There I participated as an actor and as creator and director of some programs which came to have considerable audiences. Later I became pastor of one of the small churches on the outskirts of San Jose, where my new wife had been serving. It was literally a small mission, with only fifteen full members and an attendance of about 70.

The place was called Calle Blancos (White Street, although at the time the streets were unpaved and far from white). There was no electricity or public transportation to the plaza where the church was located, so the believers walked. When I was named pastor I had the nerve, or the ignorance, to tell the believers that the work was the responsibility of us all.

"If any of you are not willing to work, better go to another church," I said. And I gave them a few addresses.

The first Sunday I was nervous, especially because a few minutes before the appointed time nobody had arrived. When Don Moises and his wife, Mary, and their boys, Fernando and Moises Junior, showed up, my soul was encouraged. Eventually a good group appeared.

When they heard my ideas, they challenged, "What do you want us to do?"

"Whatever you think best," was my reply, "as long as we maintain a good testimony and the church grows."

One man immediately suggested, "Let's have a soccer game with those who are playing in front in the plaza." Another said we should concentrate on prayer, passing entire nights crying out to the Lord for lost souls.

I agreed without comprehending all that was implied, but I soon got the idea when Carlos proposed that we hold prayer meetings once a week from 9 at night to 6 in the morning. In the church where I was converted our idea of a prayer vigil was from 9 to 12 midnight; I had never done it all night. But I went along with the recommendation.

I told them, "I'll do what you people want as long as we keep close to the Lord, do not water down the message, and stick together in spirit and action." To keep my word I had to play soccer with them on Sunday. I still remember that when we finished the first game (fortunately our team won), one of the Christian young people said, "Well, we played with you; now it's your turn to play with us in Sunday School."

Surprise! All of them, sweaty and not too clean, came in to the little wooden chapel and sat down to listen.

Later the believers in Calle Blancos decided we should try to get electricity for the area, and we succeeded even though it meant a confrontation with the town's leader of the state religion, Catholicism. Years earlier the community had requested that he take care of the necessary transactions but for some reason he had never finished.

So we went house to house, talking to the people about the need for light. Finally we held a community meeting at which time the people decided the evangelical pastor should direct the project. And soon the area brightened up.

Total mobilization of the believers in Calle Blancos, using their own methods, provided us with approximately 300 per cent growth in the first nine months. Offerings quadrupled. We bought a piano to replace our wheezy little pump organ, sent a student to Bible Institute supported by the church, installed the electricity in the community, and succeeded in having the bus line extended out to the plaza where the church was located.

In general terms we grew, and very nicely, in my opinion, although about 99 per cent of the people were very poor. Don Moises, the chief deacon, was the man with the greatest financial possibilities, and his job was selling combs.

The Lord did it all, through the believers who simply responded to the challenge to share the great things God had done for them and how He had shown mercy.

Chapter **3**

Trained in a Variety of Disciplines

Later, in 1958, thanks to Kenneth Strachan, I participated as an associate evangelist with Billy Graham in what was called the Caribbean Crusade. In other words, evangelism in all its forms has been my only occupation. For some time I was director of the Latin America Mission's division of evangelism, I have been an evangelist for 36 years, and I still am in every sense of the word.

God has honored me with the privilege of seeing thousands of people come to the altar to repent of their sins or spiritual coldness. I have taken part in great evangelism consultations, been a publicity director, and for more than 25 years have written materials on an international level regarding the salvation of souls. Since 1966 I have taken part in all the International Evangelism Congresses except one. I have been a coordinator for events such as Billy Graham's Spanish rally in New York City in 1957, when 14,500 people jammed the Madison Square Garden. I have preached in children's campaigns, been vocal soloist, songleader, pastor, bookseller, magazine editor.

Everything that contributes to evangelism, I have supported. Thanks to the Lord because He has always given me success. But the greatest ministry, the one which supersedes all these other attempts at evangelization, has been Evangelism in Depth, a name coined by Dr. Strachan and to which he gave birth, although I must confess that it has never been easy.

6

Chapter 4

Pressures and More Pressures

W hen this idea of total mobilization on an interdenominational level was officially launched, we did it in Nicaragua, where results are still evident. Dr. Rolando Gutierrez Cortes, now a well-known Baptist pastor in Mexico City, at the time pastoring a church in Managua, the Nicaraguan capital, has told me, "I continue carrying out Evangelism in Depth. It is still the best I've known."

So it was there that the Lord led us to carry out the first experiment with Evangelism in Depth. We organized prayer groups, carried out training en masse for all the church, visited house to house, sent groups to open new missions throughout the country, were forced into a controversy with the "evangelists" sent out by the Catholic church to counteract our efforts, debated publicly with priests versus evangelical pastors in the Baptist church pastored by Agustin Ruiz, organized traditional evangelistic campaigns, had pastoral retreats and even all-night prayer sessions such as in Calle Blancos. I remember a long discussion with my boss regarding the latter, because he was convinced it would be a failure if scheduled for the entire night.

Actually, it was the beginning of a whole new era in evangelization and church growth.

But it was not an easy task. Dr. Strachan had to wrestle against torrential winds and storms for the cause of Evangelism in Depth; his closest associates asked him questions which he felt had no answer. Tension among mission leaders finally got to the point that in 1961 he was told to suspend everything regarding EID.

One time he came to Guatemala and stayed at the Maya hotel. We were planning to carry out another EID experiment there and we talked a long time. He brought me instructions not to go ahead. But as his representative I had already reached an agreement with the Evangelical Alliance of Guatemala, which at that time was led by Don Santiago Villanueva, a visionary who gave everything, much more than what I can describe, for the cause of Evangelism in Depth. His wife, Angelita, even lost her health because of it.

Kenneth and I were convinced of the value of EID; its success was impossible to calculate. We were in the midst of this dilemma when a cablegram arrived from a great man of God, lawyer Jacob Stam of New Jersey, which read: "Tell Juan to go full steam ahead Evangelism in Depth."

Once again we had the green light to go forward with the third total mobilization effort, since Stam was at that time president of the board of trustees of Latin America Mission.

Don Kenneth objected to my calling EID programs experiments, and I imagine that none of the other team members liked it either, but I consider that they continue to be experiments, because no two are alike. The depth of Evangelism in Depth cannot be found outside of the local culture where this philosophy is carried out in the form of a program. When the basis, the presuppositions, and the principles are in correct order, everything else functions well, regardless of the sequence in which the program operates. It is always different.

The success of EID in Guatemala, our third country, led to later involvement in Honduras, Colombia, Venezuela, Ecuador, Bolivia, and the Dominican Republic.

I owe a great deal to Kenneth Strachan. I owe him the privilege of having considered me as national coordinator of Evangelism in Depth. He catalogued me as his friend and one day he even called me his younger brother. As the book *Who Shall Ascend?* by Elizabeth Elliot attests, his sincerity and love for the cause of evangelism became mine. Evangelism gave him both joy and anguish. In my case, because of God's call, I have always loved it and have never encountered an insurmountable obstacle to carrying it out.

One day he arrived and told me, "Juan, I was just in Founder's Week in Chicago at Moody Bible Institute and they asked me if we are really visiting house to house here in Guatemala."

"What did you say?" I replied.

"Well, I said yes," he said, "but I confess that I felt uncomfortable."

"You shouldn't doubt it," I assured him. "The work is being done with that goal in mind."

Not satisfied, he demanded concrete proof. So I suggested he select any part of Guatemala he would like to visit, in order to prove that we were working with that goal firmly in mind. He chose the north and so we drove toward Quezaltenango.

On the way a tire went flat. While we stopped to change it, two men appeared from a nearby mountain and asked for a ride. "If you wait, we'll be glad to take you," we replied.

They tried to help with the tire and we noticed something special in their presence. Back on the road again, Dr. Strachan asked them, "May I inquire what you men are doing?"

Their reply was immediate. "We are believers, working with Evangelism in Depth. For the last month we have been going from village to village visiting house to house, telling people about Christ and leaving literature.'' They then proceeded to try to evangelize us. We had to stop the car in order to weep a little from sheer joy.

God had given the answer.

Chapter 5

The First Experiment

Before we began the experiment in Nicaragua, we programed four days of Bible study, prayer, and communion among all the denominational leaders and pastors. We planned to finish with a full night of prayer. Lester J. Soerheide, a visiting writer, penned a report from which I excerpt the following:

"We went on through the four days and finally came down towards the end. And there we had one of the finest experiences ever. On the last night there was an all-night prayer meeting. About 11 o'clock we all gathered in the arbor and began singing. The service closed the next morning somewhere between 5 and 6. I thought it would drag, but it didn't. There were times of testimony, there were long periods of prayer, there were times of song, there were messages. The very last thing, just as daylight was becoming clear all around us, we had the Lord's Supper together — nationals and missionaries from twelve different groups, worshipping together in the sacred communion.

"The testimonies, many of them, were interesting. One particularly was a boy who had been converted just two weeks before, and was now our night watchman. As we slept he was constantly marching around the camp to guard us. At the other end of the spectrum, you might say, was the vice-president of the Bank of Nicaragua, a very earnest Christian. He got up, and one of the things he said was this:

" 'I thought I had been doing all right for the Lord. I was busy in my church. I had given a lot of time. But I suddenly realized tonight that what I was giving was really left over. I'm not going to do that from now on. From this minute I am giving Christ first place, and the bank and all the rest of it can take what's left over.'

"I said to myself, believe me, if we get a few more people like that in Nicaragua or anywhere else, people who will reestablish the priority in that way, nothing in the world can stop the Kingdom of God from arriving in Nicaragua."*

Well, that last night was anguishing for me. Don Kenneth and I were like midwives trying to help the birth process, although I imagine he felt we were trying to deliver twins. Following the all-night prayer time we planned to finish with a united Communion service at 6 a.m., led by Dr. Strachan, but that morning we were in the midst of a tremendous battle.

About 4 a.m. a group of Baptist pastors decided they could not take Communion with the others. An older pastor from a church outside Managua headed the group, and of course his attitude upset the last two hours of the vigil. It was up to me to deal with them alongside the bank official mentioned by Soerheide, who was president of Evangelism in Depth in Nicaragua, man of God, impassioned believer in evangelism. Without his help and that of his wife, Maria, EID would never have taken off as it did.

The situation was difficult. Dr. Strachan was already preaching the Communion message and the group of pastors still indicated their unwillingness to take it with the other denominations. I kept in touch with Don Kenneth, sending him signals to keep preaching, to give us a little more time, because the problem was still unresolved. Suffering internally, he tried to fill in the time appropriately.

The night of prayer had been unusually beautiful. Testimonies from participants in the preceding four days of classes and messages were fabulous. I still recall the two lines of people, one on each side, because everyone wanted to testify about what God had done in their hearts as a result of the ministry of Kenneth Strachan, Ramon Cabrera, John Thomas and others.

Finally about 5:30 a.m. the dissidents were moved by the Spirit of God, thanks to many prayers, and they agreed to go forward with the rest of the brethren and receive the Communion. As the bread was distributed, the whole company seemed to be in tears. We wept because the Lord had helped us defeat the enemy who wanted to divide us.

The common cry was "Glory to God!" We wept for joy. We wept with incomparable happiness.

Evangelism in Depth, by team members of Latin America Mission, Moody Press, 1961, pages 53 and 54.

Chapter **6**

The Miscarriage

In another country, I suffered miscarriage with Evangelism in Depth. The program was moving ahead full steam. God had provided sufficient Bibles to saturate a large part of the country, thanks to the World Home Bible League. More than 8,000 churches were involved, according to national coordinator Regino Palazuelos.

But there were difficulties. One day I drove to a meeting attended by all the pastors of the group presided over by Brother Samuel, who accused me of being a modernist because I loved the brethren from other denominations.

I indicated that my purpose in visiting the meeting was to deliver enough Bibles for his group to do the house to house visitation in their assigned areas. After about six hours, he sent a message asking me to put my request in writing. I was glad to do so and wrote, "We wish to place Bibles in your hands at one dollar each, for distribution. Remember we are in Evangelism in Depth."

For some strange reason, that was precisely the year he was to be president of his denomination, and he punished us hard.

One, two, and three days went by. I realized something had gone wrong in our communications, and with a friend's help I went inside the sanctuary and sat down discretely during a business session. A few moments later I was courteously asked to leave.

Finally I could take it no longer. Three days of waiting was ridiculous!

To be honest, I was upset when I walked up to the president when he came out of the meeting and I said, "Brother Samuel, I do not understand why you do not give me an opportunity to deliver these Bibles and present this matter to the pastors."

(In a way, three days was not such a long wait; one denomination took fourteen years to allow me to pray in one of its churches.)

With much supposedly Christian elegance, the pastor stared at me. We were standing on the stairs, with him above me. Suddenly he said firmly, "Move aside. You have nothing to do here; you are an ecumenical." And he shoved me to one side. His surprising action made me lose my balance and I banged my shin bones hard.

That night I went outside and wept bitterly, accompanied by Andres

Patino, a believer whom the Lord used to comfort me. During about two hours I could not stop, nor he either. It was a painful wound, not so much physically as emotionally.

Then another scene. I had been invited to preach that night by the local pastor, and he had me seated on the platform, but the president sent word to have me taken down. I went and sat in the front row below. Then the pastor protested and said I should have remained on the platform.

When I explained, he exclaimed with perplexity in his voice, "But that can't be! I'm the pastor here!"

So I returned to my chair behind the pulpit. When it was time for my participation, Brother Pedro asked me to sing a hymn before preaching. The congregation, knowing nothing of the situation, indicated their approval of the idea by their Hallelujah's and other expressions.

I felt my heart was broken when I stood up to sing, but announced I would try "No One Ever Cared For Me Like Jesus." I remember the organist played the introduction but I was unable to start. The second time, and with much difficulty I managed to sing the first verse, but on the chorus I was too emotional to go on. The burden was too heavy. I felt like the apostle Peter as I stood there and wept bitterly.

When I raised my head, everyone in the church, about a thousand people, were on their knees and faces, crying out to God. For me? No, for the Lord's work. Years later the same Brother Samuel who made me suffer so deeply, corrected his mistake, invited me to his church, offered me a meal at his table, and introduced me as his friend!

All of us preach the concept that we are one family in Christ, but almost no one practices it. Even those whose ministry is to seek unity in the body of Christ, forget that cooperating with others in the evangelistic task is not optional; it is a direct command from the Son of God which implies eternal results. Christ says we should work together "so that the world may believe." Almost everyone is willing to do it if his own organization or program is on top and receives benefit. They want to play with their own toys and they are not willing to share.

I remember on one occasion when an international organization removed all our materials from their campaign and used their own.

Cooperative evangelism is very painful, so not everyone tries it. I am among those who believe that Kenneth Strachan lost his life because of the evangelization of Latin America, and that his emotional and mental suffering upset his body balance, producing his premature death from Hodgkins disease. Without doubt he suffered agony for the lost souls on this continent, and God allowed him to see a little. He tasted the contradiction.

God has also given me that privilege, so much so that during 25 years my closest friends and associates abandoned me. I asked for their help many times . . . and their silence nearly finished me.

Chapter 7

The Strachan Legacy

Kenneth Strachan said that the growth of any movement is in direct relationship to the success that it achieves in mobilizing all its membership in constant propagation of its faith.

When he and I commented on these things, we would talk frankly for long periods of time. I questioned whether mobilizing all the membership in constant propagation of the faith would resolve the ever-present problem, because evangelism would continue to be at the mercy of external stimuli. I tried to tell him it meant accepting an external and, up to a point, violent action, because its origin came from outside the direct participation of the believer and of the Christian community.

When I had opportunity to teach classes on Evangelism in Depth, I attempted to mention these doubts "wisely" when speaking about the philosophy of the movement. Other team members laughed and decided I was eccentric; perhaps I was. What they found a pleasure, I found worrisome. I continued to believe that concentric activities were a brake to the most effective evangelism.

The best example occurred in the Appalachian mountains in Kentucky, where a totally "exported" EID was tried. The power and stimulus of total mobilization was reduced to the action of a very few who did all they could, but results were minimal. And so we were able to put some thoughts together to serve as guides for future activities.

We understood that it would be much more difficult and painful than the practice of a concentric evangelism, but finally we became convinced that if we did not take certain factors into consideration, Evangelism in Depth would never go beyond being just another program. As a matter of fact, some people still identify it this way today; others say EID has gone out of style.

Here I must mention that one determining factor in my continued participation with Evangelism in Depth was a chance encounter with Dr. George Peters, of Dallas Theological Seminary. One day he saw me in the Dallas airport and said something like this, "Juan, those boys who are in Costa Rica need your help. Kenneth is gone. You are the only one who can tell his heart. Evangelism in Depth is a good thing. It needs a lot of improvement but it is a good thing."

He took my hand, stared at me hard, his eyes damp, gave me another tight handclasp and challenged me, "Pitch in, Juan, pitch in."

Kenneth Strachan had passed away and somehow a great hole had appeared in EID leadership. By that time I had returned to my home country, Mexico, to live and work. I had left the team because of deep convictions that I should concentrate my efforts in Mexico, where the church has no legal status. The government owns the church buildings; theoretically the government of each state decides how many religious ministers may serve in its entity; religious meetings are forbidden outside of church buildings. Pastors and ministers cannot vote. In my view they are third class citizens, because even prisoners are allowed to vote.

Historically, this situation harks back to a time when the Catholic church owned 75 per cent of the good land, controlled a large part of Mexico's monetary wealth, and dominated politically. But the truth is that times have changed and there is a need for a different approach to this problem.

This state of affairs is very shameful for my country, but it has existed for more than 100 years and so far we have not found an honest leader who can change it, for fear of losing power, I imagine. The conflict between the Catholic church and the government continues. The church generally emerges on top and their permanent confrontation produces negotiations which make it appear that the government controls the church and that the church allows such control. The result is a cruel ambivalence that ends up with a people who enjoy breaking the law and a government which has to give in, even though it is supposedly supreme.

The policies followed both by church and government provide an example which is harmful to the general population. As a matter of fact, the result is more and more corruption. The government forbids religious teaching in the schools, for example, but some 35,000 private Catholic schools teach religion every day of the school year, in defiance of the government which "knows nothing about it."

Absolutely everyone is affected by this, but the principal harm is to the government, since the leaders do not realize that conditions which prevailed in the time of Benito Juarez during the last century have now changed. The truth is that the rule of Article 130 in the Mexican Constitution should be revised.

Chapter 8

Before Starting An Experiment

Those of us who were working in evangelism and understood the problems from various angles, agreed regarding certain factors needing to be considered previous to starting any evangelistic experiment. I do not have these ideas in any particular order, but this is the way I wrote them from the beginning. They could be called, "Realities of the Evangelical Church in Latin America," because Evangelism in Depth is a product of this historic moment among the Spanish-speaking peoples who, from the beginning, learned to receive, not to give. As a result, their creative capacity was nearly annulled, and they adopted models which they are still following.

Here is my list of factors to be analyzed. I trust it is clear and helps you to reflect a bit:

1) Generally few leaders and believers are interested in New Testament evangelism, in the sense of feeling it is urgent, and having a clear vision of the church's present condition.

2) The believers lose their natural ability to evangelize in direct proportion to their involvement in the technology of the church regarding personal evangelism. In other words, the more we train them in evangelism the less they do it.

3) Church members and their leaders prefer to work in well-defined programs, generated by outside stimuli, rather than accepting and reflecting about their own cosmic responsibility.

4) Christians frequently are mechanized (programed) regarding giving their testimony, because the individual initiative and innate ability which God gives to the new believer have been eliminated due to the cyclical style of training.

5) Believers often become discouraged because of their leaders' example; their lack of interest and the absence of a sense of urgency can be contagious. In many cases they seem to be ruled by a phrase like, "Teacher . . . we saw a man driving out demons in your name and we told him to stop, because he was not one of us."

The sectarian spirit in this sense is prevalent. People forget Jesus' reply to that complaint: "Do not stop him . . . no one who does a miracle in my name can in the next moment say anything bad about me, for whoever is not against us is for us" (Mark 9:38-40).

6) Unconsciously, church leaders live in a state of frustration because even though they teach many people to share the good news of the Gospel, they always end up being a discouraged minority which is awakened and involved only when there is an external stimulus of some kind.

7) Budgets for evangelism, which should be the principal task of the church, in most denominations are the smallest.

8) When told to evangelize or verbalize the message, most believers stage a slow-down strike with "feeble arms and weak knees," as pictured in Hebrews 12:12 and Isaiah 35:3.

9) The theology of evangelization is centered in the church building and in the pulpit and not the pew. However, the Lord says, "But you are a chosen people, a royal priesthood, a holy nation, a people belonging to God, that you may declare the praises of him who called you out of darkness into his wonderful light" (I Peter 2:9), and "You did not choose me, but I chose you to go and bear fruit — fruit that will last . . ." (John 15:16).

10) Contemporary evangelism lacks greater effectiveness because decisions are made at top levels, ignoring the participation of the community of believers. (Note that we are not speaking only of church members.) In reality, what this means is that if people want to be saved, they should wait until we decide officially to give them an opportunity to hear the message of salvation; and in all probability that will be some Sunday morning at 11 o'clock.

11) Because of the guilt they feel for not sharing their faith, the believers frequently take refuge in a new world (limited to other Christians), and therefore much of the time they are not aware of the spiritual needs of their community.

The church becomes a security blanket, but also a form of martyrdom, because the members hear repeatedly that they should "go into all the world and preach the Gospel." Their disobedience to the Great Commission leads them to hide and avoid having nonconverted friends.

What really happens, in my view, is that they rebel against having to use tools to evangelize which are not their own. They are Davidic in their practice, although they do not realize it. It is a natural means of self-defense, the result of an awareness of their disobedience to God.

12) Although the teaching of the value of the present, of today, is clearly explained in the book of Acts, church leaders do not easily recognize this principle for the local congregation.

In the New Testament, methodology and semantics are movable. We read of healing a crippled man, of challenging the authorities, of giving Sapphira over to Satan, of caring for social needs. Everything is mobilized without altering the content of the message, or the requirement of holy living.

13) The church no longer appropriates the promises of the Lord Jesus Christ in regard to the evangelization of the world. (See Ephesians 3:20, I Timothy 1:7, Matthew 28:16-20, John 14:12.)

14) The church no longer is the center of power where God's works are manifested. And finally,

15) Evangelism is directed by technicians, instead of men and women full of God's power. Technology has supplanted importunate prayer, compassion and urgency. I have the impression many times that those who teach have never learned and therefore they do not practice their own teaching. The pattern established by Christ in Matthew 9 has no substitute in its order, content, and sense of spiritual duty:

"Jesus went through all the towns and villages, teaching in their synagogues, preaching the good news of the kingdom and healing every disease and sickness. When he saw the crowds, he had compassion on them, because they were harassed and helpless, like sheep without a shepherd. Then he said to his disciples, 'The harvest is plentiful but the workers are few. Ask the Lord of the harvest, therefore, to send out workers into his harvest field' " (verses 35-38).

Chapter 9

Invited to Switzerland

Many years ago, through God's mercy, I was invited to Switzerland. At that time 30 men from different parts of the world met for ten days to discuss world evangelization. We talked of many things. We even spent an entire day analyzing the invitation at the end of an evangelistic sermon: how to do it, why, when, how to avoid manipulating the people, and so on.

Several participants described their methods and the success they produced, but I confess we did not pray as we should have. According to the agenda we were to tangle with the needs of the world, but we contented ourselves with dialogue and declarations. I undoubtedly sinned more than the others.

I am ashamed to say this, because I formed part of the group, but I believe a sense of urgency and compassion was absent. The world and its evangelization was like a romantic phrase, quickly passed over. The end result was to continue with what I would call a canned evangelism. I say it to my shame.

We made declarations. That was all. Yes, I realize that we need to reflect and discuss, but we also should agonize over the lost.

Chapter 10

Christ's Modus Operandi

J esus did not rest on his considerable renown. According to Matthew 9:35-38, he went from town to town, seeking out the lost and preaching the Gospel. He healed physical infirmities as well as every emotional and spiritual distress among the people. He sought them out because of the people of his time, like those of today, wandered like sheep that had no shepherd.

For Him, they were not simply away from the Kingdom of God; they were outside of it. If only the Church of today would return to its first love and follow His example! The world would once again see Christ incarnated in our passion for individuals and for souls.

I firmly believe that one point for beginning to reach the world consists of the following: that those who are in charge of our theology accept that there is one indubitable fact in the church and in the revelation of the Scripture. What is that fact? That from the very moment of his conversion to Christ and regardless of any external circumstances, God gives the new believer the capacity to handle eternal truths in an adequate way, above all, adjusted to the needs of the person who receives his message.

The determining factor in evangelism is not the Christian but the non-Christian, in order for God to select the method to be used.

God does more than His share, one might say, to guarantee that the non-Christian world have no excuse. His capacity to identify an individual as a sinner in need of God who is his only hope, is many-sided. The unlimited grace of God, the incomparable wisdom of God, and His variegated methodology are permanently in action. Day after day, God does not wear out His creativity. He never needs to repeat ideas or methods, for as we discover in Ephesians 3:20, God ". . . is able to do immeasurably more than all we ask or imagine."

Thus the total mobilization of all believers is necessary for testimony. I believe that just as the sun comes up day after day, so the qualitative and quantitative growth of the church is in direct relationship to the success that we have in teaching the ordinary believer that when it comes to sharing the message of salvation, in the moment when he is willing to give testimony, he is more capable than the professional communicator.

It was hard for me to understand this principle, but the longer I live the more I am convinced that there is a big difference between teaching and training. Training, in the sense of repeating concepts or practicing activities, is necessary in certain areas, for example in learning to play a musical instrument. But in regard to evangelism, this type of training dislocates the individuality of the person, eliminates his natural creativity, and traumatizes him. For that reason, when we methodize the church members, we also transfer to them a high percentage of guilt, because once we teach them "how," they tend to become mechanized.

If someone does not respond as expected to the established pattern, the witness becomes frustrated and distances himself from this most beautiful practice of the Christian life, which is, of course, sharing what great things God has done for him and how He has had mercy on him.

If you could take the time to investigate this principle, you would easily find thousands and thousands of trained people who have "self-destructed" in regard to witnessing. They no longer try to talk about the Lord. Furthermore, any time they attempt to do so fills them with terror and shame.

In the secular world, the opposite is often true. The more a person is trained, the more he produces. But in evangelism the situation is reversed, because the quality of the communication is the prerogative of God. For our part we must obey and keep the equipment clean and connected.

Chapter 11

The Gift Which Does Not Exist
in the Bible

An important part of this problem also resides in the fact that frequently the gift of evangelist is confused with what others call the gift of evangelism. This way of thinking simply justifies irresponsibility and disobedience.

People tend to say, "I don't have the gift of evangelism and therefore I can't share my faith in an active way."

When I hear that I think to myself: How then are we supposed to understand the Scripture that says, "You did not choose me, but I chose you to go and bear fruit — fruit that will last" (John 15:16)?

It may seen hard to understand, but in the Bible, particularly in the New Testament, there is no such thing as the gift of evangelism, nor methods with which to evangelize.

Modern evangelists often do not free their listeners to evangelize; rather they train them to bring people to the campaign. The dimension is nearly forgotten which the apostle Paul mentions in Ephesians 4:11-14, speaking of the gifts for the perfection of the saints:

"It was he who gave some to be apostles, some to be prophets and teachers, to prepare God's people for works of service, so that the body of Christ may be built up until we all reach unity in the faith and in the knowledge of the Son of God and become mature, attaining to the whole measure of the fullness of Christ. Then we will no longer be infants, tossed back and forth by the waves, and blown here and there by every wind of teaching and by the cunning and craftiness of men in their deceitful scheming."

Of course, in order to be an evangelist one must have personality, charisma, a certain degree of self-confidence and leadership so that others are willing to work on the team. Organizational and speaking ability, oratory, vision, a clear mind, and the power of persuasion through the power of God are required. I agree that not everyone has the gift of evangelist, but I declare that all believers have the natural capacity through the power of God to share what He has done for them. But they do not do it!

As a matter of fact, when someone is truly converted, he or she immediately begins to testify with great success on every level of relationships.

He or she does not ask how, when, to whom, with what materials, or whatever, but simply testifies as naturally as a little child breathes after arriving in the world and receiving a little pat from the doctor.

So it is that the new believer, touched by God, initiates the task in a natural and effective way. Evangelism is his or her lifestyle.

Paul's words in II Corinthians 5:17 have many more dimensions than those we see on the surface: "Therefore, if anyone is in Christ, he is a new creation; the old has gone, the new has come!"

To be born anew implies the acquiring of whole new capabilities.

Chapter 12

Different Schools of Evangelism

Here I believe it will be valuable to mention what we refer to as different schools of thought with regard to evangelism. Actually I will mention five, but there are only four, since the last one really is not a school of evangelism, even though it is easy to identify.

1) **Concentric.** We will begin with the concentric school. Essentially it means the multiplication of listeners. Everything revolves around a personality or a certain point of support. This type of philosophy or school of thought determines what is to be the center of the action. It revolves around an organization or an economic power. It selects the time or the times of harvest. It multiplies listeners, not communicators.

It is seldom possible for everyone to participate on the same level. A concentric campaign is expressed more in terms of an event than a process.

It stimulates dependence, even in the follow-up. The results may appear to be abundant and on various levels, but in reality there are few results, although of course they are more than what an anemic paralyzed church normally produces.

I am speaking from personal experience. I am an evangelist, and I have not stopped preaching by God's grace. In the beginning of my ministry we tried to train people to evangelize. We showed them how to smile, to knock at the door, to begin a conversation and all the rest. Results were always feeble, compared with what can be achieved by total mobilization.

Back in 1954 I expressed some of these conclusions in the hymn, "Our Country Shall Be For The Saviour," revealing my concerns and my idea of total mobilization. I wrote it in Argentina, in the room in Tandil where Kenneth Strachan was born.

2) **Cyclical.** Another school of thought is the cyclical, around which many evangelistic activities may be grouped. Today this is characterized by a sequence of events. The course of the process is predetermined.

It seems that the organization should fix the order in which God ought to act. This can fall into the frigid hands of administrative charts and plans. It assumes that if the process is carried out in an orderly fashion, the results will always be the same. There is scarcely any denomination which does not train its people to evangelize, but . . . the people do not act.

This plan ignores, up to a point, that because of the liberty with which the individual has been gifted of God, he or she is likely to rebel against everything that does not provide room for private action, for his natural way of being, such as when he first believed in Christ and expressed his witness with the dimension of his first love.

3) **Analysis and Projection.** Probably the most deeply rooted in our time is the Analysis and Projection school of thought in evangelism, because it helps those who do not wish to obey the Lord's commandment to rationalize their inactivity.

By the grace of God, some years ago I began to notice certain truths in my Bible regarding verbalized testimony that I wish to share with you, because in all these passages the Holy Spirit covers every area of our being. This dynamic can be related to physical fatigue and to the need of reconciliation with God. It is on a par with "I will make you fishers of men." It is placed in the position of greatest value and shown to be the natural activity of the new believer.

In other words, there are intellectual, emotional, spiritual, and eternal dimensions. Let me show you.

In Matthew 11:29-30 Jesus says, "Come to me, all you who are weary and burdened, and I will give you rest. Take my yoke upon you and learn of me, for I am gentle and humble in heart, and you will find rest for your souls. For my yoke is easy and my burden is light."

In Isaiah 1:18 God invites us: " 'Come now, let us reason together,' says the Lord. 'Though your sins are like scarlet, they shall be as white as snow; though they are red as crimson, they shall be like wool.' "

In Mark 1:17 the Lord calls, "Come, follow me, and I will make you fishers of men."

In Isaiah 55:1 He tells us, "Come, all you who are thirsty, come to the waters; and you who have no money, come, buy and eat! Come, buy wine and milk without money and without cost."

And also in John 4:29 the Samaritan woman uses the same verb form to call the people of her village: "Come, see a man who told me everything I ever did. Could this be the Christ?"

In each of these cases, the divine dynamics are present. Action is simultaneous with the invitation.

In the Spanish language the verb "to come" (Venid) can be separated into syllables which clearly indicate the dynamics of the Most High. In English we have something similar. For example, we say, "Come in," which indicates a state of things. We also say, "Come on," which may be an invitation or a reproach, depending on the tone of voice. "Come along" implies the responsibility not only of getting closer, but of continuing on, following the orders of the one we decide to accompany.

The fact is, God calls us and sends us at the same time.

Therefore, when we speak of Analysis and Projection, we feel obliged to emphasize that this school of thought confuses the gift of evangelist with the gift of evangelism (although this latter gift does not exist).

This form of thought projects the image of a sadistic God. Although He knows that His children do not have the capacity of obeying, He orders them to conquer the world beginning in Jerusalem, Judea, Samaria, and unto the uttermost part of the earth. Then He whimsically gives some the privilege of having the gift, while leaving the majority frustrated, unable to be happy again because they are incapable of responding to the mandate of "Go ye into all the world and preach the Gospel to every creature."

Obviously, this is not the character of the God of the Bible! Something is wrong here!

It would be easier, as I said earlier, to solve the problem if the gift of evangelism existed. But it does not. At least it does not appear in the New Testament, even by implication.

On the other hand, sadly enough, this school of thought also accepts tacitly that God has a policy of alienation, giving to some and not to others. Furthermore, it assumes that the gift of evangelism does exist. With all due respect to those who believe in this school, I believe it goes against the most elemental principles of biblical interpretation.

In this regard, it is very difficult to reconcile this idea with the mandate of the Great Commission, given to all believers with the same responsibilities and dimensions, and then intentionally — as some people believe — deny the vast majority of believers the opportunity of successfully sharing their faith.

Of course! This way of thinking inspires church leaders to make a socio-economic projecton of the work of evangelism, voluntarily ignoring that God calls "the lowly things of this world and the despised things — and the things that are not — to nullify the things that are" (I Corinthians 1:28).

Because of this, He has given all of us two things: the ministry of reconciliation and the word of reconciliation. The first refers to the understanding of the concept, and the second is the practice of this vital ministry.

4) **Centrifugal.** There is one other school, the Centrifugal, which we will leave for later.

A careful examination of II Corinthians 5:13-21 reveals some beautiful truths. Let me quote the entire passage:

"If we are out of our mind, it is for the sake of God; if we are in our right mind, it is for you. For Christ's love compels us, because we are convinced that one died for all, and therefore all died. And he died for all, that those who live should no longer live for themselves but for him who died for them and was raised again.

"So from now on we regard no one from a worldly point of view. Though we once regarded Christ in this way, we do so no longer. Therefore, if anyone is in Christ, he is a new creation; the old has gone, the new has come! All this is from God, who reconciled us to himself through Christ and gave us the ministry of reconciliation: that God was reconciling the world to himself in Christ, not counting men's sins against them. And he has committed to us the message of reconciliation. We are therefore Christ's ambassadors, as though God were making his appeal through us. we implore you on Christ's behalf: Be reconciled to God. God made him who had no sin to be sin for us, so that we might become the righteousness of God."

For example, we read that "Christ's love compels us" to declare the salvation message, "because we are convinced that one died for all, and therefore all died," and so on.

Then in verse 18 we find, "All this is from God, who reconciled us to himself through Christ." He forgave our sins through the expiatory death of the Lord Jesus. "And (He) gave us the ministry of reconciliation . . . And he has committed to us the message of reconciliation" (verse 19).

I used to believe this was an institutional mandate, but I thank God that one day He showed me how this truth was intimately related to the Great Commission, where the Lord says, "Go ye into all the world and preach the Gospel to every creature."

This command was given to all of us. The early church understood it that way and put it into practice, with a little prodding from the waves of persecution that swept over it. Christ said to them, "All authority in heaven and on earth has been given to me. Therefore go and make disciples of all nations, baptizing them in the name of the Father and of the Son and of the Holy Spirit, and teaching them to obey everything I have commanded you. And surely I will be with you always, to the very end of the age" (Matthew 28:18-20).

The Great Commission as we find it in the four Gospels gives priority to the spoken testimony as a daily practice.

This commission is given to all believers with the same responsibility and privilege that God had indicated. Jesus said, "As the Father has sent me, I am sending you." And "As the Father has loved me, so have I loved you. Now remain in my love," as well as "Anyone who has faith in me will do what I have been doing. He will do even greater things than these, because I am going to the Father" (John 20:21, 15:9, 14:12).

In other words, He tells us to go and preach the Gospel with all the power, all the time, in all nations, with all His presence, every day, everywhere. No wonder Paul exclaimed, "For I am compelled to preach. Woe to me if I do not preach the gospel" (I Corinthians 9:16).

For this reason it is sin if we do not share the Gospel, for "Anyone, then, who knows the good he ought to do and doesn't do it, sins" (James 4:17). A double sin is committed by those who dare to teach that giving the salvation message is something wicked. Although you may not believe me, there are people who teach that everything registered in the book of Acts has no validity today. As Paul said, "Let him be accursed" (I Corinthians 16:22 NKJV).

If all this is true, then there must be another answer for the fulfillment of the Great Commission, don't you think? It is impossible to accept a sadistic God. Let us seek more light in the following passages.

Chapter 13

The Basics

Let's see, for example, what Matthew reports in chapter 10, verses 16 to 20. Many people think of this type of passage as referring only to persecution, which may often be the case, but if we analyze verse 16 we see that it has to do with the task of evangelism.

Here is the text: "I am sending you out like sheep among wolves. Therefore be as shrewd as snakes and as innocent as doves. But be on your guard against men; they will hand you over to the local councils and flog you in their synagogues. On my account you will be brought before governors and kings **as witnesses to them and to the Gentiles.** But when they arrest you, do not worry about what to say or how to say it. At that time you will be given what to say, for it will not be you speaking, but the Spirit of your Father speaking through you" (emphasis mine).

Note the phrase "I am sending you out." Of course He advises us to be wise as serpents and innocent as doves, but the underlying truth is that all this happens because God wants to give these people a testimony, as we see further on.

Furthermore, He immediately brings in a universal dimension when He says, "to them [the Jews] and the Gentiles."

Now according to this passage, what should we do? What truths should we accept? Let's begin with this: "Do not worry about what to say or how to say it. At that time you will be given what to say, for it will not be you speaking, but the Spirit of your Father speaking through you."

Extraordinary that Christ insists that when it is a matter of giving testimony, the first rule is not to worry!

But what is the first thing that occurs to us when we want to share our testimony? Exactly the opposite! We suffer because we become anxious about how to begin and what to say. Read the passage carefully: "Do not worry. . . ."

In other words, the technology and the "what" are God's problem. Our problem is lack of obedience. The way to testify is something the Holy Spirit will give us "at that time." The what, the how, the when are in God's hand. The "who" is all ours.

Something else must be pointed out in this passage: "for it will not

be you speaking, but the Spirit of your Father speaking through you."
So in this case we are simply channels. Our responsibility is to keep the
equipment clean and properly connected to the power source so that the
message will not be disfigured or distorted but clear, thanks to our clean
life and our communion with the Lord. Or, as Jesus puts it, our fellowship with the Father.

Here, if you prefer to see your life as an instrument, you are correct.
As human beings we can never communicate with the mind of the spirit
of someone else. Therefore, every time we send out a message, regardless of what it may be, or under what circumstances, it will be defective.
But in the moment in which we send it out, the Holy Spirit intervenes,
codifies it, makes it adequate and understandable.

Thus when it reaches the hearer it arrives with the meaning which
the other person, the non-Christian, needs to understand. That's why
the Lord says, "Do not worry." As a result, many people are helped
by the words or actions that we do not even remember saying or doing.

But let's go on, examining other passages that are directly related
to the word of reconciliation, our testimony. Here is Mark 13:10,11:
"And the gospel must first be preached to all nations. Whenever you
are arrested and brought to trial, do not worry beforehand about what
to say. Just say whatever is given you at the time, for it is not you speaking, but the Holy Spirit."

Comparing these two passages, we find some ideas repeated. For in-
stance, "it is not you speaking, but the Holy Spirit." And "say whatever is given you at the time." Also, "do not worry beforehand."

But there are still other dimensions that are very important and up
to a point progressive. Let's examine them carefully.

In Mark, the Lord uses even more inclusive language than in Matthew, when He says, "the gospel must first be preached to all nations,"
including the religious and political world. The verb is "must" and the
objective is "all nations." But when we get to this point, He adds, "do
not worry beforehand about what to say."

Do you see the emphasis? Here the Holy Spirit goes deeper. When
He says, "do not worry beforehand," He refers to a situation that we
know about; we do not merely have a vague concern. And He adds,
"about what to say," implying our will and our understanding. It is one
thing to repeat phrases, and quite another to say things of our own free
will. This is the emphasis I want you to see.

The interesting thing here is that it doesn't matter what position we
may be in, either as conductor of the conversation or as participant, the
Lord's advice is the same: "Do not worry beforehand about what to
say." The quality, form, and content of the testimony are God's prerogative. Marvelous!

Let's turn to another passage dealing with our testimony, Luke 12:8-12: "I tell you, whoever acknowledges me before men, the Son of Man will also acknowledge him before the angels of God. But he who disowns me before men will be disowned before the angels of God. And everyone who speaks a word against the Son of Man will be forgiven, but anyone who blasphemes against the Holy Spirit will not be forgiven.

"When you are brought before synagogues, rulers and authorities, do not worry about how you will defend yourselves or what you will say, for the Holy Spirit will teach you at that time what you should say."

Here the Lord is clearly speaking of the need of testifying as a result of our conversion. I refer to verses 8 and 9. Interesting, too, that in referring to our testimony the Lord mentions the unpardonable sin. Might this mean that we should not judge the work of the Spirit in the non-Christian? I leave this conclusion to you.

But I do want to point out the fact that here the Lord clearly refers to synagogues, rulers and authorities, while insisting, "do not worry about how you will defend yourselves or what you will say." I see a third dimension here that I would like to explain.

One is "what you should say will be given you at that time." Another: "Say whatever is given you at that time." And the third: "Do not worry about how you will defend yourself or what you will say."

In other words, the Holy Spirit's help is there, whether we are on the defensive or the offensive. If we need to defend our faith, the Holy Spirit becomes our teacher par excellence. If we must declare the good news or denounce sin or demonstrate man's condition before God, "the Holy Spirit will teach you at that time what you should say."

Isn't that fabulous? Doesn't that make you feel as though a heavy load had fallen from your shoulders with regard to testifying?

Yes, the Holy Spirit does it all. But He gives us the credit. He's a great motivator!

Some years ago in Seattle, Washington, I was invited to go on a fishing expedition for salmon. We left Seattle to sleep near the wharf, and about 4 a.m. we began fishing. Radio announcements told us where to navigate and I recall that we spent the whole morning going back and forth. Several men in the party caught salmon, some early, others later, but I caught nothing.

Bernie, one of the Christian men in the group, noticed my predicament and offered, "Lend me your rod." He took it in his hands, threw it with all his might, and in what seemed like seconds shouted, "Juan, we've caught something! Grab the rod! Let it out! Now draw it in so the fish bites firmly! Turn it! Don't let him pull away!"

And finally a beautiful salmon appeared on the line.

Everyone shouted, "Look what Juan took in!" Several congratulated me heartily. But of course Bernie was the one who deserved the credit.

Many times I have thought that this is a perfect example of what happens in evangelism. The Lord does the work and mercifully gives us the credit, because He is the One Who prepares the situation and works things out so that people may have the opportunity to hear the Gospel.

Luke 12:11,12 brings out another factor. The situation here is violent. We do not find the element of testifying to others, but the Holy Spirit repeats, "When you are brought before synagogues, rulers and authorities, do not worry about how you will defend yourselves or what you will say, for the Holy Spirit will teach you at that time what you should say."

Let me ask: Do we need any better teacher when the Lord assures us that the Holy Spirit will guide us? Let us not forget that God's thoughts are wiser and higher than ours.

The apostle Peter reminds us, "For prophecy never had its origin in the will of man, but men spoke from God as they were carried along by the Holy Spirit" (II Peter 1:21). Whenever the Spirit intervenes, the message will be right. It will be God's Word!

One other passage should be shared here, Luke 21:13-15. This one completely finished off my inferiority complex.

I recall an occasion several years ago when I was traveling to Mexico. The trip was lengthy, so there was opportunity to chat with my seatmate, and he detected almost immediately that I was a pastor. The same thing has happened on other flights.

Another time I was in Brownsville, Texas, with my wife and son, Juan David, when an elderly couple came up to me and asked, "You are Christians, right?"

"Yes we are. How did you know?"

"We saw you hold hands and pray for the food."

Experiences like these help me to behave myself better, because I never know who may be observing me, although of course the most important thing is to remember that God is present everywhere.

At any rate, the person I mentioned on the plane began talking with me about different subjects and in every case he knew more than I did, so I began to feel it was useless to talk any more with him. People seated all around us were listening and some looked at me with pity as if to say, Poor pastor! I must admit I would have appreciated being swallowed up about that time, or at least having a different seatmate.

When we were about to land, he stood up in the aisle and said in a voice loud enough to be heard by everyone, "Well, pastor, we are about to separate, and according to you we'll never meet again because you're going to heaven and I'm going to hell."

Before that happened, I had thought to myself, "This man knows more than I do about philosophy, literature, and history, but he probably knows nothing about the Bible." However, as I had attacked him with verses and biblical concepts, he had come back with, "The verse you are quoting does not say that in the original . . . ." My attempts at giving testimony seemed null and void, not only because I had been ridiculed, but also because I felt inferior. I couldn't even use the tools I felt comfortable with!

So at the end of our ride together, I said, "Never mind, they won't even accept you in hell."

"What did you say? What do you mean by that?" he retorted.

"I'll be glad to explain what I mean," I replied. And so I had my chance to give testimony after all.

That experience provided me with an excellent background for Luke 21:13-15 (NKJV). Here it is:

"And it will turn out for you as an occasion for testimony. Therefore settle it in your hearts not to meditate beforehand on what you will answer; for I will give you a mouth and wisdom which all your adversaries will not be able to contradict nor resist."

Understand that I am not talking about improvising in our tasks of teaching or preaching. I am not talking about the knowledge that we need in order to grow. I am speaking about what God does when we need to witness for Him.

Here we close the cycle. The Holy Spirit says that when we wish to tell about the things God has done for us and how He has been merciful to us, we should not be anxious. We should not worry! We should not meditate beforehand how to answer!

Remarkable, don't you think? The basis of all this is our testimony to others, although my heart rejoices when I read here, "Therefore settle it in your minds." This is an inclusive concept. "I will give you a mouth and wisdom, which none of your adversaries will be able to withstand or contradict . . . ."

This promise and this reality are for all believers. How marvelous! Paul was right when he wrote, "I can do everything through him who gives me strength" (Philippians 4:13) and "We are more than conquerors through him who loves us" (Romans 8:37).

As I said before, in the moment of our conversion God gives us the capacity to handle eternal truths adequately, but above all, adjusted to the need of the receiver.

Chapter 14

Changing Hearts Without Surgery

Once when traveling from Houston to Mexico City I walked into the international waiting room and began talking with a pleasant young man. Later on the plane he asked me, "Excuse me, what is your occupation?"

"What do you suppose it is?" I answered.

"Well, you have the appearance of a doctor," he ventured.

"You're right," I said. "I'm a specialist."

"In what field?"

"I change hearts without the need for surgery."

"Really? How do you do that?"

"Well, it's a long complicated process. You'd probably find it boring."

"No, sounds interesting! I've never heard about that."

"Are you sure you want to hear? It is quite dull."

"I don't care. We have plenty of time since the flight is long."

Since he insisted, I proceeded to tell him that God can change a heart of stone, insensitive to His voice, and transform it into a heart of flesh, tender to God's call. Then I showed him the verse in I Samuel 10:9 where "God changed Saul's heart."

Flying at an altitude of 37,000 feet I said, "We're right high in the sky here. Wouldn't you like to have God change your heart?"

He answered in the affirmative, and we bowed our heads together. I put my hand on his shoulder and at that instant the stewardess came by and asked if someone was ill. "Do you need any help?" she inquired.

"No, I am just changing the heart of this young man."

Later on she came by again and said, "Excuse me, but a while ago I asked if you felt ill and you said you were changing his heart. Did I hear correctly?"

"Yes, that's right," I replied. "Would you like to know how I did it?" The Lord gave me the opportunity of talking to her about Jesus as well.

Oh, if we would only hold on to the promises of God with regard to giving testimony! "Open wide your mouth and I will fill it," He promises in Psalm 81:10, and "The mouth of the righteous brings forth wisdom" in Proverbs 10:31.

A Christian lady whom I respect highly, told me one day when I was telling her about these experiences, "Do you know what I do? I visit house to house and tell the people I have some lessons that take 30 days. Give me 30 days and I'll teach you how to get into hell without any problem." Very unorthodox method, but she claimed it brought results!

Pastor Reina of Aguascalientes, Mexico, has been greatly used of God. One time during an Evangelism in Depth program he gave the following testimony:

"I generally carried a large Bible with the photo of Pope Paul VI. When I knocked on a door, I showed them the photo and said I'd like to take a few moments of their time to talk about the ideas printed in this book approved by the pope."

He assured me that with such a method no one closed the door on him.

Chapter 15

Mr. Engineer, You Are An Ignoramus

Luisa was a Christian who won an engineer named De la Torre to the Lord. He is an unusually capable man who, in addition to his profession, speaks five languages. When he told me he was fluent in English, Italian, French, and Arabic in addition to Spanish, I was tempted to laugh. But I swallowed my doubts, thanks to various testimonies from people who spoke those languages and after I met a Brazilian believer who also spoke five.

When I finally met the engineer and asked how he had been led to Christ, he replied dryly, "They called me an ignoramus."

"Really? Who would say such a thing?"

"Luisa, our family servant."

Then he explained. "Luisa can scarcely read or write, but every day for a year she would say to me, 'Sir, you are ignorant because you have not read the Bible.' She insisted so much that I finally decided to open the Bible just so she would stop insulting me. And you know what happened."

Today he is pastor of a flourishing church.

In other words, **the number of methods of communicating the Gospel of salvation are multiplied as many times as people are willing to share and have opportunity to do so.**

One time a friend of mine was walking toward his church in a Latin American city. A neighbor who made fun of his faith saw him leave and asked where he was going.

"I'm going to a place for real men," answered my friend Antonino.

"Really? Can I go along?"

"I doubt you are sufficiently manly to go in. You're too much of a coward."

"If it's a place for real men, I'm going," insisted the neighbor.

"All right," said Antonino, "but I'm warning you it's only for real men."

"I already understood that!" exclaimed the friend.

"Then come along. You won't be sorry you did."

When they arrived at the evangelical church Antonino started in the door, but the neighbor balked. "Are you going in there?"

"Of course," said Antonino. "Only real men enter this church. Since you are a coward, I knew you wouldn't make it."

"I'm no coward!" shouted the frustrated neighbor.

"Then go in," challenged Antonino. "Prove it." The poor neighbor felt cornered and went in. That night he accepted the Lord as his Saviour.

We read in II Timothy 1:7, "For God did not give us a spirit of timidity, but a spirit of power, of love and of self-discipline." And in Jeremiah 1:9 the Scripture says, "Then the Lord reached out his hand and touched my mouth and said to me, 'Now, I have put my words in your mouth.' "

In His sermon of comfort in John 14:25,26, Jesus tells His disciples, "All this I have spoken while still with you. But the Counselor, the Holy Spirit, whom the Father will send in my name, will **teach** you all things and will remind you of everything I have said to you."

When I read this passage I feel that the age of the computer really began in that upper room. Here is the beginning of a memory that can be used at any time; the only difference is that a computer is still dependent on its operator. Nevertheless, what I wish to emphasize is that the Holy Spirit will teach us all things and will bring to our remembrance everything Jesus has said to us.

Imagine that! The playback capacity is infinite. The Holy Spirit will continue in control of the communication of the salvation message.

We must remember that Christ has reminded His disciples once again that He is the way, the truth, and the life. He has said He and the Father are one, a concept which is not easy for the disciples to digest. Thomas inquires, Jesus replies. Jesus states that He will ask the Father to comfort the disciples with the Holy Spirit and He says, "But you know him, for he lives with you and shall be in you" (John 14:17b).

So when we approach the marvelous experience of sharing our testimony, of speaking of Christ, there is nothing to fear. The Spirit will teach us everything if we are properly connected with the center of operations, our Lord Jesus Christ.

Have you considered the riches accumulated in your brain due to all the ideas that you have heard about the Kingdom of God and about His glory since the day you first gave your heart to Christ?

Of course I wish to make it clear that in no way am I fostering irresponsibility or the improvisation which is so prevalent and easy to imitate. No! God has given us common sense and has taught us to maintain discipline in our devotional life. Furthermore, Peter says, "But grow in the grace and knowledge of our Lord and Saviour Jesus Christ" (II Peter 3:18a).

But we must never lose our perspective and understanding that the

Holy Spirit is the best evangelist. We are only the means.

Note, for example, this passage from John 16:7-15:

"But I tell you the truth: It is for your good that I am going away. Unless I go away, the Counselor will not come to you; but if I go, I will send him to you. When he comes, he will convict the world of guilt in regard to sin and righteousness and judgment: in regard to sin, because men do not believe in me; in regard to righteousness, because I am going to the Father, where you can see me no longer; and in regard to judgment, because the prince of this world now stands condemned.

"I have much more to say to you, more than you can now bear. But when he, the Spirit of truth comes, **he will guide you into all truth.** He will not speak on his own; he will speak only what he hears, and he will **tell you what is yet to come. He will bring glory to me** by taking from what is mine and making it known to you. **All that belongs to the Father is mine.** That is why I said the Spirit will take from what is mine and make it known to you" (emphasis mine).

What a wonder! What extraordinary things the Lord tells us here! Did you notice He says He will guide us into all truth? And that He will tell us what is yet to come? That the Spirit will glorify Christ? And that the Spirit will take what is Christ's and make it know to us?

If this is the way things are, then there is no excuse for not witnessing for Him. If He does it all, and He does it well; if He teaches us and reminds us of all we have learned, then (I repeat) the problem is a matter of obedience.

Do you recall what the Bible says is sin? Yes, it is the transgression of the law, but more profoundly, as James 4:17 says, "Anyone, then, who knows the good he ought to do and doesn't do it sins." So in our seminars of Evangelism in Depth we affirm that it is easy to evangelize, so easy that not to do it is sin.

I recall once when we were in the God is Love Presbyterian Church, north of Mexico City. We had announced that the objective of the seminar was to demonstrate that evangelism was so simple it was a sin not to do it. I hope that by now you can understand what happened when we had our evaluation session, after 25 hours of teaching, and a woman exclaimed, "At last I feel free from guilt! I finally shared the Gospel with my neighbor."

Another testified, "I had never tried to witness before, but now I invited my friends and they all accepted my invitation!"

Still another stood to say, "Brother Isais told us it was easy to evangelize. I want to say it is so easy, so simple, that here is my neighbor with us today."

That same Sunday the congregation decided as a body to renew their first love for Christ and to act the way a person does who has fallen in love.

Chapter **16**

Crazy . . . But For Love

We began to teach these principles many years ago, sharing with people and leaders that their underlying problem is the loss of their first love. When someone is in love, he will do anything. He is motivated! He is thrilled to spend time with the one he loves; he is not ashamed to be seen with the object of his love, regardless of circumstances. He sees everything as positive. There is a solution for every problem.

Some wag has stated (rightly) that our brain can scarcely distinguish between being in love and being crazy. I remember when my future wife and I went on an excursion to the Irazu volcano in Costa Rica, where we met. When we arrived at the top of the volcano, the girls in the party decided that the men ought to go down part way into the crater, where sulphuric smoke drifted up.

One of the fellows, Bill, twisted his ankle down there and could not walk. He was a well-built American, and I was a rather thin Latin, certainly not husky enough to carry Bill up to the top of the crater. The clouds were beginning to come in and it was important that we get out of there without delay.

How well I remember that when my fiancee realized the situation, she challenged me, "You can do it, dear, you can do it! Bring him out!"

I have no idea how I managed, but I brought him out. And as the years go by I have often marvelled at the craziness of what I did, all for love. Praise God I did not develop a hernia.

The first fruits of that rescue were a warm embrace and a kiss that I can still taste. Which brings me to say that there are certain characteristics typical of people in love. They are easy to recognize, but let me list them here.

First, of course, it is important to mention that many people confuse their passions with love, and so once they obtain the carnal satisfaction of their passion they go back to their old ways and the marks of true love are not present very long.

The characteristics of love are quite evident. One is that the person needs absolutely no external motivation to speak of the object of his adoration; he mentions it at every opportunity, appropriate or not. Everyone in the vicinity knows he is in love.

He may be in a room where someone comments on the beautiful white mums decorating the table, and he raptures, "They remind me of Mary's eyes." Have you ever seen a girl with white eyes? But all he can think of is Mary.

Do you see what I am driving at? The important thing is to share the love we feel. I am in love and I want everyone to know about it! It is romantic to talk about the person I love.

A second characteristic of a genuine love affair is that the person wants to spend as much time as possible with the other. Once the couple is married and it occurs to the husband to add up all the hours he spent with his wife before the big day, he realizes he could have studied for a masters degree or a doctorate in that much time. And if you ask the couple what they talked about all those hours, they look at one another in wonder. The important thing was just to be together.

A third characteristic is that the person in love is willing to do things that he'll never do again. Imagine a couple in the north country in winter with the temperature at zero degrees when the girl says, "My love, I think it would be fun if you went out with just your undershirt and walked a couple of miles. I'll go with you."

He replies, "Of course, that's a great idea." And when he is nearly frozen to death and she asks him if he is cold, he insists, "No, I feel warm, darling."

Or the couple might be in Acapulco with a temperature of about 95 degrees in the shade and he says, "I'd love to see you in your new fur jacket."

"Really, dear?" That night she wears it to dinner and feels perfectly cool, just to please her love.

That is what it means to be in love. It is openly demonstrated, it takes time, it includes taking risks, it requires making an effort and yet it is romantic, delightful, satisfying.

If you make a careful study of the book of Acts, particularly the first six verses of chapter 17, you will find an historic reality. For the apostle Paul, testifying of Christ was as natural as eating every day. The Bible records it this way:

"As his custom was, Paul . . . ." It was his lifestyle!

Here is the passage in full.

"When they had passed through Amphipolis and Apollonia, they came to Thessalonica, where there was a Jewish synagogue. As his custom was, Paul went into the synagogue, and on three Sabbath days he reasoned with them from the Scriptures, explaining and proving that the Christ had to suffer and rise from the dead. 'This Jesus I am proclaiming to you is the Christ,' he said. Some of the Jews were persuaded and joined Paul and Silas, as did a large number of God-fearing Greeks and not a few prominent women.

"But the Jews were jealous; so they rounded up some bad characters from the marketplace, formed a mob and started a riot in the city. They rushed to Jason's house in search of Paul and Silas in order to bring them out to the crowd. But when they did not find them, they dragged Jason and some other brothers before the city officials, shouting: 'These men who have caused trouble all over the world have now come here, and Jason has welcomed them into his house. They are all defying Caesar's decrees, saying that there is another king, one called Jesus.' "

Later I am sure you remember that Paul risked the death penalty or terrible corporeal punishment when he taught that there was another king besides Caesar, but wherever he went he fearlessly declared that Jesus was the Savior. He was willing to do anything for the cause of Christ!

That's why the people of Thessalonica complained, "These men who have caused trouble all over the world have now come here." They were not rioters nor agitators in the modern sense; they were believers in love with their Lord who proclaimed that the Savior had been raised from the dead. For them, Christ was not an historic figure but a living reality that could not be silenced.

Paul's words to the Thessalonians in I Thessalonians 1:5-8 reveal how these believers continued in their first love and practiced total mobilization:

"Because our Gospel came to you not simply with words, but also with power, with the Holy Spirit and with deep conviction. You know how we lived among you for your sake. You became imitators of us and of the Lord; in spite of severe suffering, you welcomed the message with the joy given by the Holy Spirit. And so you became a model to all the believers in Macedonia and Achaia — your faith in God has become known everywhere. Therefore we do not need to say anything about it."

Also: " . . . your faith is growing more and more, and the love every one of you has for each other is increasing" (II Thessalonians 1:3b).

The genuine answer for the fulfillment of the Great Commission is the believer's return to his first love, because when there is love, the lover is willing to face the consequences of his love. Not that it is reasonable or logical, because as the saying goes, "Love has reasons that reason does not understand."

Let us return now for a moment to the wisdom of the Holy Spirit as regards our testimony. Paul speaks of human wisdom, saying that it is not very useful in evangelism, since what counts is "not with wise and persuasive words, but with a demonstration of the Spirit's power, so that your faith might not rest on men's wisdom, but on God's power" (I Corinthians 2:4,5).

He also refers to God's "secret wisdom, a wisdom that has been hidden," which is also ours because God decreed it "for our glory before time began" (verse 7). It was not understood by any of the rulers of this age, but God has revealed it to us by His Spirit because the Spirit searches everything, "even the deep things of God" (verse 10b), and this tremendous passage in I Corinthians 2 goes on to say that "this is what we speak, not in words taught us by human wisdom, but in words taught by the Spirit, expressing spiritual truths in spiritual words" (verse 13).

For this reason, Paul does not hesitate to correct our perspective as regards to evangelism. Listen to what he tells us:

"But to those whom God has called, both Jews and Greeks, Christ the power of God and the wisdom of God. For the foolishness of God is wiser than man's wisdom, and the weakness of God is stronger than man's strength.

"Brothers, think of what you were when you were called. Not many of you were wise by human standards; not many were influential; not many were of noble birth. But God chose the foolish things of the world to shame the wise; God chose the weak things of the world to shame the strong. He chose the lowly things of this world and the despised things — and the things that are not — to nullify the things that are, so that no one may boast before him. It is because of him that you are in Christ Jesus, who has become for us wisdom from God — that is, our righteousness, holiness and redemption. Therefore, as it is written: 'Let him who boasts boast in the Lord' " (I Corinthians 1:24-31).

In the light of all this, we can draw only two possible conclusions. If God had left the fulfillment of the Great Commission entirely in our hands, the Gospel never would have gotten further than Jerusalem. On the other hand, should God have decided to do it without us, He would not have the joy of proclaiming that His creation (we) had been restored to His image.

He does it all, yet He needs our human clay which He models according to the need of the hearer, because He deeply loves the souls of the lost from eternity to eternity.

In Latin America a favorite chorus goes,

"I want to be, oh Lord, like clay in the potter's hands.
Break my life, make it over; I want to be a new vessel."

Our verbal testimony of what God has done for us, with Christ's miraculous birth, His death in our place, and His resurrection as the center of our message, is the only answer for humanity and for the Church.

When the apostle John was in God's presence according to Revelation 12:7-12a, he tells us:

"And there was war in heaven. Michael and his angels fought against the dragon, and the dragon and his angels fought back. But he was not strong enough, and they lost their place in heaven. The great dragon was hurled down — that ancient serpent called the devil, or Satan, who leads the whole world astray. He was hurled to the earth, and his angels with him. Then I heard a loud voice in heaven say: 'Now have come the salvation and the power and the kingdom of our God, and the authority of his Christ. For the accuser of our brothers, who accuses them before our God day and night, has been hurled down. They . . . .'

Now take note: " ' . . . They overcame him by the blood of the Lamb and by the word of their testimony.' " Do you see it? By the word of their testimony!

We go on reading, " ' . . . they did not love their lives so much as to shrink from death. Therefore rejoice, you heavens and you who dwell in them!' "

Glory to God! Hallelujah! The word of their testimony is indestructible. That's why the Spirit says to the churches, not only the one at Ephesus, but to all churches, "Yet I hold this against you: You have forsaken your first love" (Revelation 2:4).

Love is the key. "Dear friends, let us love on another, for love comes from God. Everyone who loves has been born of God and knows God. Whoever does not love does not know God, because God is love" (I John 4:7,8).

Our first love shows us that we have a tremendous responsibility to share the Gospel truth. Just like the Old Testament lepers, we reconsider the situation and conclude, "We're not doing right. This is a day of good news and we are keeping it to ourselves. If we wait until daylight, punishment will overtake us. Let's go at once and report this to the royal palace" (II Kings 7:9).

Of course, when we pay no attention to our responsibility and ignore the fact that we are mandated to come and go in a double action, "we're not doing right." The prophet Ezekiel puts it strongly when he says,

"The word of the Lord came to me: 'Son of man, speak to your countrymen and say to them: When I bring the sword against a land, and the people of the land choose one of their men and make him their watchman, and he sees the sword coming against the land and blows the trumpet to warn the people, then if anyone hears the trumpet but does not take warning and the sword comes and takes his life, his blood will be on his own head. Since he heard the sound of the trumpet but did not take warning, his blood will be on his own head. If he had taken warning, he would have saved himself. But if the watchman sees the sword coming and does not blow the trumpet to warn the people and the sword comes and takes the life of one of them, that man will be taken away because of his sin, but I will hold the watchman accountable for his blood.'

"Son of man, I have made you a watchman for the house of Israel; so hear the word I speak and give them warning from me. When I say to the wicked, 'O wicked man, you will surely die,' and you do not speak out to dissuade him from his ways, that wicked man will die for his sin, and I will hold you accountable for his blood. But if you do warn the wicked man to turn from his ways and he does not do so, he will die for his sin, but you will have saved yourself." (33:1-9).

Let's look at the apostle Paul's familiar words. "All have sinned and fall short of the glory of God . . . for the wages of sin is death" (Romans 3:23, 6:23). This is true! Our friends, our relatives, our fellow workers, our neighbors are all condemned to eternal death.

That's the way it is. Ezekiel says, "The soul who sins is the one who will die" (18:4c). Therefore, it is impossible to understand the Great Commission without accepting the fact that God enables us to be true watchmen, guardians for Him and for men, from the very moment of our conversion. We are the answer.

Chapter **17**

The Missionary of Decapolis

I'd like to invite you to examine one more biblical example. This is Jesus' praxis, found in Mark 5:1-20. Let me quote the whole story:

"They went across the lake to the region of the Gerasenes. When Jesus got out of the boat, a man with an evil spirit came from the tombs to meet him. This man lived in the tombs, and no one could bind him any more, not even with a chain. For he had often been chained hand and foot, but he tore the chains apart and broke the irons on his feet. No one was strong enough to subdue him. Night and day among the tombs and in the hills he would cry out and cut himself with stones.

"When he saw Jesus from a distance, he ran and fell on his knees in front of him. He shouted at the top of his voice, 'What do you want with me, Jesus, Son of the Most High God? Swear to God that you won't torture me!' For Jesus had said to him, 'Come out of this man, you evil spirit!'

"Then Jesus asked him, 'What is your name?'

" 'My name is Legion,' he replied, 'for we are many.' And he begged Jesus again and again not to send them out of the area.

"A large herd of pigs was feeding on the nearby hillside. The demons begged Jesus, 'Send us among the pigs; allow us to go into them.' He gave them permission, and the evil spirits came out and went into the pigs. The herd, about two thousand in number, rushed down the steep bank into the lake and were drowned.

"Those tending the pigs ran off and reported this in the town and countryside, and the people went out to see what had happened. When they came to Jesus, they saw the man who had been possessed by the legion of demons, sitting there, dressed and in his right mind; and they were afraid. Those who had seen it told the people what had happened to the demon-possessed man — and told about the pigs as well. Then the people began to plead with Jesus to leave their region.

"As Jesus was getting into the boat, the man who had been demon-possessed begged to go with him. Jesus did not let him, but said, 'Go home to your family and tell them how much the Lord has done for you, and how he has had mercy on you.' So the man went away and began to tell in the Decapolis how much Jesus had done for him. And

45

all the people were amazed.''

After reading this biblical event, in your mind answer the following questions:

Who is the principal actor here?
What was the real condition of this man?
Did he find a solution to his problems?
Once he was liberated, what was his greatest desire?
What was Jesus' reply?
What was the order?
What was the method?
What was the geographic area?
Was the man successful?

I suggest you answer all these questions going back to the text. When we examine the passage, we discover that Jesus' negative reply does not seem to make sense. I imagine that the first time the formerly possessed man begged the Lord to let him go along with the other disciples, Jesus' voice was probably normal. But when he insisted the second time, I feel that Jesus' tone increased in volume, "I said no! What you must do is go and tell your people the great things that God has done for you and how he has had mercy on you.''

He says the same to us.

Chapter 18

In Practical Terms,
What Is Evangelism in Depth?

From the point of view of program, Evangelism in Depth is the mobilization of all the believers to give testimony of their faith, within the framework of the local church, using local leadership and with global objectives.

Frequently, of course, those who take our courses want us to dedicate one class period to explaining what it is. In case my readers have the same concern, I will try to give you a synthetic version in a few words.

In practice, Evangelism in Depth is:

1) **Joining resources together in order to multiply results.**

When a few people do a great deal, all their efforts amount to little. But when many people each do a little, their small efforts add up to a lot. This idea is well expressed in the theme hymn of Evangelism in Depth, which says,

"All our country shall be for the Savior
If together we battle for Him.
All the nation shall honor the Savior
And show forth His great power over sin;
To the task, then, with holy devotion,
Preaching Christ to the lost everywhere!
Loyal Christians, unite! Save our land for the right!
For our Lord will soon be here!

"From the north to the south and all over,
East and west need to hear about Him,
It's the message that offers redemption
From sin to a new life in Him.
In every town, every house, every city
We must preach about Christ everywhere.
Yes, they all need to know He can save them from sin
And soon He'll come again!"

2) It is teaching linked to practice.

The "come" and the "go" are completely linked. There is no separation either in time or in space, because the love of Christ constrains us. Come and go, the permanent theme of the Lord Jesus Christ.

3) It takes the Christian back to the romance of his first love.

This happens when he returns to the days when talking about the Lord was his lifestyle, without any external stimulus.

4) It is reorientation of our perspective regarding evangelism.

The Great Commission has been given to all. The complementary ministry of all the members of the body of Christ, must be understood and practiced. Christians can and should work together in evangelism. If we are going to be together in heaven, we might as well get used to being together here.

5) It is the Christian's new attitude which remains even after the official Evangelism in Depth experiment has ended.

By experiment we mean program, because when the foundation, the presuppositions, and the principles are firmly in place, the program changes from one place to another even within a single country. Remember that the depth of Evangelism in Depth cannot be found independently of the culture where this philosophy in the form of a program is carried out.

Evangelism in Depth is centrifugal force that begins with the individual, according to Acts 1:8, and continues with him regardless of any external circumstance. It is simultaneous movement toward God and toward men, believers or nonbelievers. The only way to prove that we love God is to love our neighbor as we love ourselves. This is the sum of the law of God.

6) It frees the believer from his bad habits.

I refer to his spiritual life, so that he may express his faith in a natural, spontaneous way. Experience has taught us that the believer who is highly methodized, suffers from spiritual paralysis. He is handicapped.

7) It transforms the believer and he becomes the pastor's right arm.

Pastors need fewer stars and more team members.

8) **It is agonizing prayer and a systematic program of action, adjusted to the local culture, combined in equal proportion.**

Please note that we are not saying organized prayer, although this is also needed. We speak of agonizing in prayer for the salvation of the lost. When the believer agonizes, God reorganizes values, people, resources, nations, ideas, everything!

9) **It is practicing the ministry of reconciliation, given to all believers according to I Peter 2:9, John 15:16, and II Corinthians 5:11-21.**

10) **It is changing men in order to change structures, or changing the unit in order to have a better community.**

I believe we should also note here that Evangelism in Depth is not proselytizing in depth; that is the recycled school of evangelism. It is not a traditional evangelistic campaign. It is not contemporary philosophy. It is a school of thought whose results remain throughout the ages, because God has promised that the very gates of hell cannot prevail against the Church, that is, against two or three who are meeting in His name.

Nor is Evangelism in Depth an organizational power. It simply means to put into practice the methods of Jesus Christ over against our own.

Chapter **19**

Agonizing in Order to Reorganize

Leaving this brief exposition about training the believer to share his faith effectively, we should now approach the book of Acts in order to discover its modus operandi, its principles, and the value of the present that the first Christians demonstrated for extending the Kingdom of heaven.

Let us begin with the following: "They all joined together constantly in prayer, along with the women and Mary the mother of Jesus, and with his brothers.

"In those days Peter stood up among the believers (a group numbering about a hundred and twenty) . . . " (1:14,15).

If you carefully examine this beautiful passage, you will note that the center of everything is prayer. When the Bible says that "they all joined together constantly in prayer," one can imagine their prayers. The presence of Thomas and the use of his logical arguments may have been discouraging, but Peter's firm convictions, whether or not he could explain them, counteracted Thomas.

Almost all of us who serve in Christian work have difficulty fulfilling our daily contact with the Lord through prayer. We recognize that prayer changes things. We understand that we ought and always to pray and not lose heart. We know that he who asks receives, and he who seeks finds, that he who knocks has the door opened to him. We understand that where two or three are meeting in His name, God is in their midst. We understand that the prayer of a just man has great power in its effects, and that if two or three are agreed on earth they may ask what they will and it will be done.

But . . . we don't do it! It is understandable when the very fact of having been created by God provides me with a spirit of independence and security that I try to put into practice every second. Prayer inspires me, but more often it condemns me because it is so easy to fall into hypocrisy.

When we pray we remember the sins that only God and we know about. In prayer we realize we ought to ask forgiveness of those who offend us. As we pray, our troubled conscience resounds with "Do not be overcome by evil" or "If your enemy is hungry, feed him; if he is

50

thirsty, give him drink" or "Forgive us our debts as we also have for-given our debtors."

Furthermore, the Lord says, "If you love me, keep my command-ments." Who can pray on those terms? In truth, no one! No sincere Christian can go before the Lord in prayer without ending up spiritually and physically shamefaced on the floor.

On the other hand, there is nothing more exciting than taking ad-vantage of the promises of God through prayer. II Chronicles 7:14 says, "If my people who are called by my name, will humble themselves and pray and seek my face and turn from their wicked ways, then will I hear from heaven and will forgive their sin and will heal their land."

One of the first activities to be organized in an Evangelism in Depth program is prayer. In Guatemala, for example, in 1962 we had 6,035 fully identified groups that dedicated themselves to prayer for all the year's activities, with an average of six people in each prayer cell and a team dedicated exclusively to keeping them informed about requests. Every two weeks we sent them a prayer list and a praise list, because we included requests that had been answered.

Over the years God has permitted us many beautiful experiences re-garding prayer. On one occasion in Nezahualcoyotl City, adjacent to Mexico City, a woman noticed a sign placed in the window of a believer's home which read "Evangelism in Depth Prayer Cell — Here we pray for your problems on Wednesdays at 6 p.m. Welcome!"

She asked the group, "Is this for real?"

When they replied affirmatively, she said, "I want you to pray for my aunt. Many years ago she came here and she has been lost ever since."

In the area around Mexico City thousands of people get lost every year; in fact, there is a special phone number called Locatel for report-ing cases of lost relatives or friends. The woman added, "If she can be found, I will join your group." One way of saying she would believe in Christ.

Challenged by this woman, the believers cried out to God and within one week the lost aunt appeared. Can you imagine the impact on that community?

I recall one time in Venezuela when we had a problem. We needed to travel to a certain place, but we had no money, no contacts, nothing! We spent that night crying out to the Lord and about 4 o'clock in the morning a non-Christian from down the block knocked at the door.

Somewhat fearfully the brethren opened the door, and the man said, "Tell me what your problem is. I haven't been able to sleep all night thinking about you."

We told him. He exclaimed immediately, "I'm going to lend you a truck and I'm going to fill up the gas tank, and I hope I can sleep the

rest of the night!''
    Later that week he was converted to Christ.
    Another time in Puerto Rico, in a town named Corral Viejo, I was
sharing with the congregation that the secret of God's work is prayer.
No programs, or seminars, or leaders, or materials, or courses of discipleship, not even Evangelism in Depth. It is prayer. When people pray,
persevere and beg, God opens the heavenly fountains and sheds His blessing, providing whatever is necessary for His glory.
    That Sunday night a woman was visiting from New York. After the
service she came up to me and asked, ''Do you believe God can do miracles even long distance?'' When I said yes, she explained, ''My husband is not a Christian and I have talked to him about the Lord for a
long time, but he won't accept anything.''
    ''Well,'' I replied, ''if you pray, God can do the work in a way you've
never even imagined, but you must pray believing that He hears you and
that He will answer.'' We agreed to pray early every morning for her
husband, who was a sailor.
    Monday, Tuesday, and Wednesday mornings we prayed fervently for
that request. To his wife's amazement, the man arrived in Puerto Rico
on Wednesday! He explained that the ship on which he was to have em-
barked was held up for some reason and didn't sail. He returned home,
felt lonely, remembered his wife was visiting Puerto Rico and decided
to join her. That week he accepted the Lord in the campaign.
    Many times we do not know how to pray, nor why, but the Scrip-
ture teaches that the Holy Spirit intercedes for the saints according to
the will of God, particularly when we are witnessing. Romans 8:26 reminds us, ''In the same way, the Spirit helps us in our weaknesses. We
do not know what we ought to pray for, but the Spirit himself intercedes for us with groans that words cannot express.''

Chapter 20

Who Should Die?

When we were carrying out Evangelism in Depth in the Dominican Republic, we lived through many experiences that were difficult to understand. The first week of their civil war, which started the same time as EID was officially launched, a Christian man was killed while on his knees in church, praying that the Dominican Republic (Quisqueya, as we call it) could be reached for Christ. Later it was claimed that he had been confused with a terrorist being chased by government soldiers; they thought he had gone into the church. But regardless of the official story, he died on his knees.

One experience was particularly difficult for me. Difficult to understand. Even now it bothers me and I cannot fully comprehend its significance, although when I have shared it with others, they have found it helpful.

It happened like this.

We were coming across from the side of the troops of General Wessin y Wessin. Praise God, the president of Evangelism in Depth's national committee was lawyer Alfonso Lockward, who had such a fine reputation that those of us who worked with him could move around freely, although cautiously, in spite of the war. As I neared the soldiers of the Interamerican Peace Army, one of them, tall and dark, interrogated me. When he found that I was a pastor, he said, "I'm a believer, too, a Baptist. I'm here in obedience to my country."

Then looking across at the other side of the international corridor that divided the island, he asked me, "Please pray for us. Those on the other side are communists and they must die so this island may be free."

I listened with mixed emotions, not because I was in favor or against either group, but simply because to want the death of any man, no matter who he is, does not make my soul rejoice in the slightest. It is not that I am a coward; it's just the way I am.

But when I finally crossed to the other side I found a situation that was similar but yet totally different in its meaning for me. A group of young men armed with machine guns saw me coming and said, "We know who you are. Nevertheless we warn you to be careful. We are at war! The enemy is there, across the corridor. They have invaded our country!"

Then one of them whispered, "Brother, pray for us, that God may give us the victory and we can finish all of them off."

Lord! I cried in my spirit. For whom should I pray? I tried to do some intellectual exercises — spiritual calisthenics, you might say — and finally I convinced myself that I could not pray for either of the men who called me "Brother." Anguishing!

Even now when I remember it, I sigh and thank the Lord for not asking me more than I could bear.

God has seen fit to raise up many people to help me through the years. One is Daniel Hartzler. In the beginning, when I told him some of these adventures in prayer, I could tell that he listened with a spirit of doubt. But one day we had the pleasure of being together for a campaign on the Yucatan peninsula in the southern part of Mexico.

The temperature there is extremely hot, often more than 100 degrees. When we arrived to take part in an activity related to Evangelism in Depth, the believers told us, "We've been asking God to change the climate, since we know you suffer with the heat and it will be better for us all."

The goal was to reap a harvest of souls, publicly. They even had some children trained to be counselors, as well as adults. The Philadelphia church grew in just three months from 60 people to 169, according to Pastor Severo Ek of Yucatan.

Well, we listened to the men tell about their prayer request, but we paid little attention until the climate began to get colder. The temperature went down so far that Dan had to stand and say, "Brethren, don't pray so hard. We are dying of cold!" They had asked God for cool weather through the end of the campaign on Sunday, and sure enough, by 9 a.m. on Monday when we left the town of Cordomex, it was already good and hot.

Chapter 21

The Value of the Present: Geometric Projection

I believe that the prayer of those 120 people in the first chapter of Acts went something like this: "Lord, and what are we going to do now? How are we going to restore our credibility as leaders? What are we going to do with this small group that has remained, since we don't know what has happened to everyone else? Brother Nicodemus has disappeared, and Caiphas keeps on with his threats. . . ."

Probably the ones who prayed with the greatest assurance of an answer were Mary and the women who had gone to the sepulchre. Mary would never forget the angel's message that day long ago: "Do not be afraid, Mary . . . you will be with child and give birth to a son, and you are to give him the name Jesus. He will be great and be called the Son of the Most High . . . and he will reign over the house of Jacob forever; his kingdom will never end" (Luke 1:30-33).

For her everything had not ended on the cross. She could not explain it, but she was certain that the future of these few people who believed in Jesus would soon change for the better. Nothing could destroy His work. A sword had pierced her heart with Jesus' death, but for her the taste of the wound indicated the salvation of the world.

It is interesting to note here that the Spirit approved the keeping of records. The number of 120 is valuable because it allows us to see the growth of the church so clearly that no one can possibly argue with what Luke has registered.

If we continue to chapter 2, verse 41, we find that in a matter of hours the church has grown from 120 to more than 3,000. Peter's sermon initiated in verse 15 bears unprecedented fruit. Note that it was not Peter who gave the invitation; his listeners were so cut to the heart that they cried out, "Brothers, what shall we do?"

Do you find it unusual that here the non-Christians are using the word "brothers" which signified the communion enjoyed by the earliest disciples?

Peter's message was full of power; it was not a canned speech, nor reheated. It was full of content. Peter identifies with the history of his people, with their leaders, but above all with the death and resurrection of Christ. Backed by his "team," Peter says, "This Jesus God has raised the power of the living God."

This is what we need today: the reality of the power of God in the Church, in our seminaries, in our pastors, in our members, in our programs. The Church is so mechanized that God has no part in the action. As a result, thanks to the limitations of human wisdom, as well as the obstacles administratively speaking and the lack of dependence on the Highest, people are bored.

When they arrive at church they already know what is going to happen, what the prayer will include, what hymn will be sung, how long each portion of the service will take, at what point they ought to greet each other (perhaps a bit stiffly), when they should stand, when they should be seated. There is no sense of expectation as to what God may do.

Some choruses that we sing in Latin America seem to me to contain the secret of why some churches are alive. They go something like this:

"Christ is here, ask Him whatever you like,
He has power and He will answer you.
Christ is here, friend, ask Him whatever you like.
By faith we draw near, Christ, to you
And though your face is not visible to us
We know that you are here."

So here is the difference. This contrasts with other attitudes, right? I remember one time I was to preach in a church where the pastor, a young man just out of seminary, told me, "Brother Isais, I expect you in my office at 10:45."

I arrived on time and we began to talk about the church, its problems, and so forth, but he seemed nervous. Every few moments he pulled up his sleeve and consulted his watch.

Finally I asked, "Are we in a hurry? I'm ready."

"No," he said, "it's just that we should pray three minutes before we go in. That's what the instruction book says."

What a crime! What a prisoner of the system! What ironclad, irrational dependence! Why couldn't we use the fifteen minutes to pray? Why not half an hour? This is why the church does not grow, because it is mechanized, it has no life of its own, it is depending on external stimuli.

Chapter **22**

The Golden Cage

$\mathbf{A}$ few years ago I wrote a small book which I never published because in it I had vented some frustrations and denials of certain things. The title was *The Golden Cage*. Perhaps one of the chapters is worth quoting in general terms.

The story is of a pastor who unexpectedly finds himself in the midst of an accident where there are dead and wounded. Over the sound system he hears a call: "Is there a priest or pastor here that can help? Many dying people need spiritual help."

The pastor listens to the announcement, but today is supposed to be his day off, and his wife will be upset if he does not get home. Furthermore, suppose the dying person should be of a different denomination. Besides, he could get into trouble with the police or the insurance company if he tried to lift an ill person. And he really had other plans for this day. . . .

The announcement comes the third time. He should do something! He decides to jump from the train station platform onto the tracks to get closer to the injured, but loses his balance and his briefcase hits the ground and breaks open. Everything scatters. The pastor picks it up as quickly as possible, except for his pastoral manual, and proceeds toward a twisted figure that cries out, "Help me! I'm dying!"

The pastor embraces him with his left arm, then places him carefully back on the ground because he needs the instruction book. He runs his finger down the index: How to Prevent a Divorce, How to Help a Cancer Patient, When a Couple is Childless, How to Guide in the Writing of a Will, Counseling for Drug Addicts, Counseling for Pregnant Girls Regarding Abortions, How to Reconcile Divided Families, How to Help the Poor, and on and on; but nothing about helping someone who is about to die in an accident.

He realizes he is on his own. He again places the man's head on his arm, wipes the blood from his face, looks at him with compassion and says sadly, "Friend, you must understand the value of your circumstances. God controls every situation and uses it for good. Only when we find ourselves can we find God, according to one of our most famous theologians. I invite you to pray, and you may join me in closing with

57

the Lord's Prayer."

The man dies as the pastor intones, "Lord, it is never too late to see the future. The attitude with which we face our present circumstances will give us results tomorrow. . . ."

Yes, I realize this is a caricature, but it is one way of signaling the danger of a church that is so tied to its traditions that it cannot take advantage of the present, as did the first century Christians. I am sure Peter did not sit down to consider the implications of baptizing 3,000 people, regardless of the form used to baptize them. I also doubt that he stopped to analyze the theological basis of his sermon. He saw a need that must be met immediately, he allowed the Spirit to lead him, and the early Christians followed his example. No wonder they grew so rapidly.

We mentioned previously that in Acts 1 there were 120 believers; in Acts 2 there were 2,120. Now check Acts 4. Verse 2 indicates that the disciples were emphasizing the resurrection once again. We must remember that circumstances were adverse at this point. The religious leaders were against the Gospel and violence threatened, yet the church continued to grow, as verse 4 makes clear: "However, many of those who heard the word believed; and the number of the men came to be about five thousand" (NKJV).

Considering the cultural context of this passage, it is obvious that since the day of Pentecost there were already 5,000 men, and adding women and children to the total would give an even greater number. What phenomenal growth!

But for the benefit of our calculations, we will limit ourselves to the figure given for men. In the next chapter, the picture is even more encouraging. Signs and wonders motivate Jesus' followers to take possession of Solomon's Portico. They are not concerned about the acceptance of the populace nor about the rejection of the religious leaders, and we read, "And believers were increasingly added to the Lord, multitudes of both men and women" (5:14 NKJV). This seems to indicate that the church has now accepted an important social change. Women are taken into account. And the total must be very numerous for Luke to say "multitudes," don't you think?

Another important fact, the natural result of spiritual growth, is registered in chapter 6. The believers develop a social concern. Everything was done properly because they had to be "full of the Holy Spirit and wisdom" (6:3 NKJV). But in verse 7 we see something extremely interesting: the writer tells us, "And the word of God spread, and the number of the disciples multiplied greatly in Jerusalem, and a great many of the priests were obedient to the faith" (NKJV).

Now here is an immense difference: multiplication, instead of addition, which is our prevalent concept today. The Scripture says "multiplied greatly," giving us a larger dimension, not only because the ordinary believers were increasing, but also because the religious leaders were coming to believe in the risen Christ.

When we reach chapter 9 in this record by the Holy Spirit, we discover that the church has been established in Jerusalem, Judea, and Samaria as Jesus had commanded. Verse 31 explains,

"Then the churches throughout all Judea, Galilee, and Samaria had peace and were edified. And walking in the fear of the Lord and in the comfort of the Holy Spirit, they were multiplied" (NKJV).

All the churches had peace, they were being edified in the fear of the Lord, and as a result they were being edified in the fear of the Lord, and as a result they were being strengthened in the Holy Spirit. Here the multiplication principle has become an institution. Now we no longer talk about individuals, but about groups and assemblies.

Going on to chapter 11, we see that the brethren were pressured by the persecution and they scattered far and wide, even to such faraway points as Cyprus, causing some new believers from there to go to Antioch and spread the Gospel to the Gentiles there. Notice verse 21:

"The Lord's hand was with them, and a great number of people believed and turned to the Lord."

And in verse 23 we read that Barnabas went and "encouraged them all to remain true to the Lord with all their hearts . . . and a great number of people were brought to the Lord" (11:23b, 24b). Notice it was "a great number."

To get the full picture, we must go back to chapter 8, when "a great persecution broke out against the church at Jerusalem, and all except the apostles were scattered throughout Judea and Samaria . . . those who had been scattered preached the word wherever they went" (8:1,4).

We stated previously that the growth of the church is directly related to its success in teaching the ordinary believer that he is more capable of sharing the Gospel of salvation than the professional communicator, when he is willing to put it into practice. Yes, there was persecution in the early church, but that was not the secret of its growth as some people teach. On the contrary, they were persecuted because of their faithfulness and obedience to the commandment received from the Lord.

The Church need not be persecuted in order to grow. What it needs is to repent and turn away from its evil ways and obey the Lord. The problem is not our external circumstance but our heart which is rebellious to the celestial vision, not sharing about the One whom we love without having seen Him, as Peter puts it.

The problem is disobedience! But the early church was obedient, so no wonder the Holy Spirit records this definitive phrase which indicates something as natural as breathing. He says, "So the churches were strengthened in the faith and grew daily in numbers" (Acts 16:5). Daily,

daily, daily! Can you imagine? Today we have churches which lose people daily, daily, daily.

We find another expression further along which presents the same picture. "Many of those who believed now came and openly confessed their evil deeds . . . in this way the word of the Lord spread widely and grew in power" (Acts 19:18, 20).

Their only secret was their passion for lost sinners. Paul testifies to this when he speaks of what people saw in him and in his companions before they were converted. Here are his words:

"You know how I lived the whole time I was with you, from the first day I came into the province of Asia. I served the Lord with great humility and with tears, although I was severely tested by the plots of the Jews. You know that I have not hesitated to preach anything that would be helpful to you but have taught you publicly and from house to house. I have declared to both Jews and Greeks that they must turn to God in repentance and have faith in our Lord Jesus" (Acts 20:18-21).

Paul picked up this compassion from Ananias, who was his teacher and consolidated him in the faith. Ananias received it from the apostles who "daily in the temple, and in every house . . . did not cease teaching and preaching Jesus as the Christ" (Acts 5:42 NKJV).

A question I hear frequently from certain fellow workers is this: Is there any more biblical evidence to prove these ideas? Of course there is.

For example, nowhere in the New Testament do we see Christ teaching His disciples to evangelize. Nor do we find the apostles doing it. The most frequently quoted passage, Ephesians 4:11,12, has to do with the gift of evangelist and the perfection of the saints, not with the fulfillment of the Great Commission, but with growth in the Christian life.

Let me quote those verses: "It was he who gave some to be apostles, some to be prophets, some to be evangelists, and some to be pastors and teachers, to prepare God's people for works of service, so that the body of Christ may be built up."

Discipleship in the modern sense is not evangelism and much less evangelization. Evangelism means to confront the sinner with the reality of being lost eternally in hell and the possibility of being redeemed by the blood sacrifice of Jesus Christ. No matter how we tell him, or when, what matters is that he understand he is lost but there is hope.

Giving testimony through our lifestyle is useful only when we also present the message verbally. Our life supports or destroys the impact of our words, but we cannot evangelize without speaking. At least that is the style of the New Testament. Anyone who tries to alter it will find himself winning friends, but not rescuing anyone from condemnation.

Make a study of the churches where people "live their Christianity" but never talk about it. They are dying! Believe me!

Chapter 23

Altering God's Program

Evangelization requires the participation of all believers, each in his or her own way. When it comes to evangelism, an individual's "errors" are transformed by God into positive approaches that get results with personal salvation. I would like to point out two classic examples in Jesus' ministry.

The first is found in John 4:1-42, Jesus' encounter with the Samaritan woman. the text suggests that Jesus had no alternative but to pass through Samaria, for geographic reasons. In other words, in that particular moment Samaria was not His top priority. But the important thing to note is the methodology He uses.

First: He stops at Jacob's well. He knows the rules of the game and is aware that no decent person will appear at the hottest hour of the day to draw water. True, He is tired and wants to take a rest from walking.

When the woman comes into view, Jesus begins the conversation on a familiar subject. A simple question opens the door for a dialogue which deals with racism, the dichotomy with regard to worship, and the surprise of finding a Samaritan who believed none of the ideas that she had lived with all her life.

Her expression, "Sir, you have nothing to draw with and the well is deep. Where can you get this living water? Are you greater than our father Jacob?", I believe is her tacit recognition that Jesus is quite possibly the Messiah.

I am sure both the Samaritan and Jesus spoke words which the Holy Spirit did not wish to register, but which brought her to a very personal experience, because verse 15 reveals she is beginning to understand, although incompletely: "Sir, give me this water so that I won't get thirsty and have to keep coming here to draw water."

Quite abruptly Jesus tells her, "Go, call your husband and come back."

She shows Him the transparency of her situation and Jesus continues with His clear, patient message. When was the Samaritan converted? We do not know. Was it when Jesus brought her sins into the light? "You have had five husbands, and the man you now have is not your husband." Was it when she declared, "I can see that you are a prophet"?

We do not know.

But we are certain that she believed in Christ. The results of her attitude demonstrate that without any doubt.

To understand better, let's read verses 28 to 42 because they reveal Jesus' methods over against ours. John writes, "Then, leaving her water jar, the woman went back to the town and said to the people. . . .

Can you imagine the impact on the wives when they see a female like that talking with their husbands? "Come see a man who told me everything I ever did. Could this be the Christ?" She invites them to reflect on a deeply profound subject.

Then she immediately forces them to take responsibility for their thoughts. "They came out of the city and made their way toward him." Isn't it interesting that at first Jesus does not seem to pay any attention to them? On the contrary, from verses 31 to 38 He answers questions asked by His disciples. He does not miss a chance to widen their perspective.

He tells them there are better things than merely material values. He says that many people want to learn from Him, that what is needed is to begin to reap the harvest. He reminds them that no one is more important than another, when it comes to harvesting; the main thing is to be aware of the opportunity. "Open your eyes and look at the fields! They are ripe for harvest," He insists. And then comes the most beautiful revelation of all.

I call this the first total mobilization campaign. It was organized by a woman of bad repute, full of doubts, whose social status was far from acceptable, in a place where "Jews do not associate with Samaritans," and with a Jewish preacher. How about that? No wonder Isaiah records that the Lords says, "so are my ways higher than your ways" (55:9).

The most surprising aspect here is that the Samaritans, led by this new convert, alter the Lord's agenda. Before this incident the text reads, "He left Judea and went back once more to Galilee. Now he had to go through Samaria" (John 4:3,4), implying that He never intended to stop in Samaria. But His pleasure at what was happening there, motivated Him to stay two more days! John evaluates the results:

"Many of the Samaritans from the town believed in him because of the woman's testimony . . . So when the Samaritans came to him, they urged him to stay with them, and he stayed two days. And because of his words many more became believers. They said to the woman, 'We no longer believe just because of what you have said; now we have heard for ourselves, and we know that this man really is the Savior of the world'" (4:39-42).

How much instruction about the *what* and the *how* did Samaritans receive? What was the theological content of her message? Why was Jesus willing to take part in an activity where all the leaders had only a few hours of Christian experience? How is it possible that the woman, with her negative image, could motivate so many people from the city to listen to Jesus?

"Many of the Samaritans from that town believed in him because of the woman's testimony . . . and because of his words many more became believers" (4:39,41) are stated together, in the same context, with equal value. The Holy Spirit does not differentiate between the quality and content of the Samaritan woman's message and the Lord's. Naturally, the result of the latter was the more abundant, because He is the Lord of the harvest.

"The Lord has done this, and it is marvellous in our eyes" (Mark 12:11). God enables believers to share the faith successfully on any social level from the very moment of their conversion. I understand that this is hard to accept intellectually, but who can argue with the living God? Not I!

To contract His word will never be possible. Those who question it seem to go off in some direction but at the end, as Paul says, "every tongue (will) confess that Jesus Christ is Lord, to the glory of God the Father" (Phillippians 2:11).

We have said that the depth of Evangelism in Depth cannot be evaluated apart from the culture where this philosophy is carried out in the form of a program, and the Evangelism in Depth is centrifugal movement that begins with the individual and continues with him, regardless of circumstances. Perhaps the best way to explain this will be to take the example of how a hurricane operates.

According to our general knowledge about this meteorological phenomenon, the center of a hurricane is a totally peaceful spot. The sun may be shining and children playing because it is a place of absolute calm. One time Jesus said, "Peace I leave with you; my peace I give you. I do not give to you as the world gives. Do not let your hearts be troubled and do not be afraid" (John 14:27). The hurricane obtains its enormous energy from a centrifugal movement whose effects are felt thousands of kilometers away from the center, or eye, of the hurricane.

"So far we know of nothing we can do to control it," a hurricane specialist once told me. "All we can do is try to weaken it, but once it gets started it can't be stopped."

The same is true of a real believer in Christ. No one can stop him from sharing that "which we have heard, which we have seen with our eyes, which we have looked upon, and our hands have handled, concerning the Word of life . . . " (I John 1:1 NKJV).

The fact is that all new believers begin this way. Their movement is centrifugal. But then we discover they lose their natural ability to talk of what Christ has done for them, because they begin to trust more in themselves than in the Lord who does the work through the Holy Spirit's intervention. How do they lose their first love? Who ruins them?

We find a clue in Hosea: "And it will be: Like people, like priests" (4:9a). The church follows the pastor's example.

Chapter 24

The Baby Theologian

An example of this movement toward God and toward men is the testimony related by the apostle John in his ninth chapter. Before we begin to study this passage, I want to emphasize three specific realities that must not be overlooked.

For one thing, neither Jesus nor the disciples apparently had a particular interest in healing this blind man. Their concern was more theological, for they asked, "Who sinned, this man or his parents, that he was born blind?"

Secondly, according to John's story, the blind man himself showed little interest in being healed.

Thirdly, of course, the community was totally disinterested and obviously the leaders of the synagogue even less so.

But the disciples' question was a good one, and Jesus replied, "Neither this man nor his parents sinned, but this happened so that the work of God might be displayed in his life."

The narration goes on, "Having said this, he spit on the ground, made some mud with the saliva, and put it on the man's eyes. 'Go,' he told him, 'wash in the pool of Siloam' (this word means Sent). So the man went and washed, and came home seeing."

We can imagine the blind man with his outstretched hand begging, "A penny for this poor blind man," "Give me charity . . . I cannot see." As he speaks he feels someone come close, he hears someone spit, there is a brief silence, and then when he least expects it, he feels the saliva and someone anointing his eyes.

Perhaps he feels the urge to thrust Jesus away, shouting "Leave me alone! Don't interfere with my life!" But he obeys the order to go and wash, and he comes back with the ability to see.

Now come several important points to be noticed. First, this miracle caused an impact in the community. "His neighbors and those who had formerly seen him begging asked, 'Isn't this the same man who used to sit and beg?' "

Second, it divided the community into three groups. "Some claimed that he was. Others said, 'No, he only looks like him.' But he himself insisted, 'I am the man.' 'How then were your eyes opened?' they demanded. He replied, 'The man they call Jesus made some mud and put it on my eyes. He told me to go to Siloam and wash. So I went and washed, and then I could see.' "

This was his entire message. All the city was affected by it; they could not ignore his testimony.

The testimony of a believer concerning his salvation is so powerful that it goes beyond time and eternity to condemn Satan. "The man they call Jesus made some mud . . . So I went and washed, and then I could see." Here is the basic concept: "the man they call Jesus." The formerly blind man did not know that Jesus was the Son of God. Perhaps that is why his message was so simple, without any theological content. "Jesus made some mud and put it on my eyes . . . and I washed, and now I see."

This message churned up the town, and caused the officials of the synagogue to call an emergency session in which they recalled their agreement "that anyone who acknowledged that Jesus was the Christ would be put out of the synagogue." In other words, the message of the blind man made an impact even on the intellectual and religious world.

The impact was such that it could not be contradicted. The only thing to be done was defend themselves from the effective communication of the baby theologian who was changing the people's attitude regarding the carpenter's son from Nazareth.

But there are still other extremely interesting details in this story. "The Pharisees also asked him how he had received his sight," says verse 15. He replies as he had done before. Then in verse 16, "Some of the Pharisees said, 'This man is not from God, for he does not keep the Sabbath.' But others asked, 'How can a sinner do such miraculous signs?' So they were divided."

John refers here to some of the leaders, perhaps those who were more sincerely desirous of getting to the bottom of the matter.

They are divided. Now notice what verse 17 tells us, "Finally they turned again to the blind man, 'What have you to say about him? It was your eyes he opened.' "

What a profound reply they get! "He is a prophet."

All very simple, states this teacher who so very recently was initiated into the school of the Kingdom of God. Do you see who is winning the argument? The Pharisees become so anguished that they call in the blind man's parents, but the old couple refuse to cooperate. So in verse 24 we read, "A second time they summoned the man who had been blind. 'Give glory to God,' they said. 'We know this man is a sinner.' "

We must credit the Pharisees with a deep desire to discover the truth. They are confused, upset, anguished — and they want a more elaborate answer, but the former beggar is guided and taught by the Holy Spirit in that hour and with wonderful assurance he insists, "Whether he is a sinner or not, I don't know. One thing I do know. I was blind but now I see!"

The Pharisees are not satisfied. With tenacity, their pride covering their ignorance, they question him again, "What did he do to you? How did he open your eyes?" And he answers, "I have told you already and you did not listen. Why do you want to hear it again?"

Now a judgment has been established and he reproaches them, implying that their real motive is something different because they do not listen. Then incredibly, driven by the vehemence of the Pharisees, the former blind man invites them to believe! He asks dryly, "Do you want to become His disciples too?"

Who is giving the invitation? To whom? The truth of his words, his style, his correct use of language, give this believer a stature that makes him invincible. Any other words can be cast into doubt, but one's personal testimony has strength that cannot easily be destroyed. It certainly cannot be ignored.

Since the Pharisees could not contradict the experience and message of this visionary disciple, they turn to violence as their last resort. Verse 28 says, "Then they hurled insults at him and said, 'You are this fellow's disciple! We are disciples of Moses! We know that God spoke to Moses, but as for this fellow, we don't even know where he comes from.' "

The new Christian who used to be blind gets a bit sarcastic here, giving them a good punch in the liver as he answers, "Now that is remarkable! You don't know where he comes from, yet he opened my eyes."

Then, with a self-assurance that the Pharisees lack, he delivers an extraordinary four point sermon. By now he has become a leader in the community, for he speaks in plural:

1) "We know that God does not listen to sinners."

2) "He listens to the godly man who does his will."

3) "Nobody has ever heard of opening the eyes of a man born blind."

4) "If this man were not from God, he could do nothing."

His eloquence is such that I imagine the Pharisees standing there with their mouths open, becoming furious because a Mr. Nobody is giving them a class in theology, history, doctrine, and pastoral psychology. I think more than one of them was grinding his teeth in anger, but they could do nothing. His arguments were well founded, his suppositions correct and his conclusions irrefutable. As a parting shot, they insulted him, "You were steeped in sin at birth; how dare you lecture us!"

The reader be the judge. Who won the debate? A simple believer, with the help of the Holy Spirit who guides us to all truth. An ordinary believer, in love with God. A common believer who has not forgotten his first love and who is willing to do anything, because for him testifying is an easy, romantic, pleasant task.

It is always this way for the new Christian and it should be the same for all believers, regardless of the number of years we have known the Lord. If someone has no desire to share his faith, perhaps he is not a son of God after all.

The formerly blind man was expelled from the temple, but that provided him an opportunity to meet Jesus once again and see Him face to face. Before knowing Him, he loved Him, he defended Him and he talked about Him powerfully. From then on he would speak of Jesus more and more. That's the way it is. If we meet Him, we talk of Him.

In this story, the former blind man sees everything clearly . . . and everyone else is blind by the end!

Chapter 25

Profile of the Church

In modern terms, total mobilization of the church requires deprogramming and raising the awareness level in order to function normally. When we began Evangelism in Depth and had to give it an expression from the point of view of program, we listed ten factors that should be kept in mind before structuring anything. This is the background of Evangelism in Depth's origin, the way I saw it from the beginning.

First: We carefully evaluated our work in traditional campaigns. Of course, we have never been against such campaigns, nor are we now. Campaigns are good, but they are not the best method for fulfilling the Great Commission because they use a concentric method that is fabulous to break the ice, to give a sense of belonging, to demonstrate the unity of the body of Christ, to provide training, to permit a great orator to be used by God, to project a strong image, to produce immediate results from a work team . . . but they do not permit the total mobilization of the believer and his community in a centrifugal force that involves ministering to the whole man.

Second: We proposed to eliminate or at least diminish the inferiority complex of Latin American church leaders. In one of my earlier books, *The Other Side of the Coin* (published by Eerdmans), I go into this problem more fully. We live this experience time after time and it concerns us, because to a great extent it affects the development and continuation of evangelism.

Third: We wanted to show the missionary institutions all that can be done with Latin American flexibility, methodology, and optimism. We Latins do not work well with long-range planning, nor with systems that eliminate the personal touch. Friendship, spontaneity, and the value of the here and now, are essential to carrying out any significant activity that is to develop authentic roots. We also know how to work in teams where personal stimulus is not lost because of administrative policies. For that reason communism cannot prevail on this continent, except by force. As it comes, it goes.

Fourth: We also wanted to demonstrate to leaders in top administrative responsibilities, that nationals are capable of accomplishing great things when someone believes in them, when authority is really delegated to them, and when their ideas are backed in a practical way. Possibly this is one of the most difficult attitudes to preserve, because we are not well known, because in any evangelical undertaking there is a tendency to paternalism, and because this is the baggage that we have been lugging around for decades.

Fifth: Through the different Evangelism in Depth activities we also wanted to change the mentality of the leadership and of the ordinary church member regarding verbalization in evangelism, so they would accept it as a natural expression. Not only the nationals, but other Christians who serve here in Latin America are atrophied in that sense. It doesn't take long for the careful observer to discover that there are still leaders who try to be the full orchestra, killing themselves doing an endless number of jobs, who could delegate these projects to others, particularly in the field of evangelism.

Chapter 26

Musical Therapy

Sixth: In theory the Latin man is a free spirit, but in the depths of his soul he is a slave to himself and all his victories and sorrows come out in song. Knowing this, and taking into the account the dimensions of our culture, we wanted to experiment and measure the dimensions of using music to teach the theology of evangelism with regard to the concept of total mobilization.

Each of the choruses and hymns we sing has an element of correction, of teaching, and also of motivation toward evangelistic activity. Music represents a high percentage of the believer's liberation in evangelism.

Music is not only therapy, it is life. Music destroys when it is used improperly. Music is from God, and reconstructs attitudes and personalities, but when the devil directs it, symphonies become evil and deadly. Let us see some of the music used in Evangelism in Depth, observing its themes.

"Our Country will be for the Saviour." This hymn, really the marching orders of Evangelism in Depth, contains ideas that provide the new believer with a different perspective. We see it in each line:

"Our country will be for the Saviour" — a broad global objective.

"If together we battle for Him" — the biblical modus operandi, the entire body of Christ working together.

"All the nation shall honor the Saviour" — exalting Christ's sovereignty.

"And show forth His great power over sin" — reflecting the thought of Zechariah that it is "not by might nor by power, but by my Spirit, says the Lord Almighty" (4:6b).

"To the fight, then, with holy devotion" — this line calls for action, based on holiness before the presence of God.

"Preaching Christ to the lost everywhere" — here the area to be reached is the world. It is the practical response to the Great Commission.

"Loyal Christians, unite, Save our land for the right!" — the call to work with a nationalistic spirit, one Lord, one Spirit, one baptism, but also with an awareness of responsibility, recognizing that all of us in the Lord's family are part of the solution, working with a truly Christian attitude.

"For the Lord will soon be here" — in this last line, the sense of urgency is clearly expressed. We do not "run like a man running aimlessly; [we] do not fight like a man beating the air" (I Corinthians 9:26), but we fight with the definite hope of Jesus' coming again for His people. It is impossible to have evangelistic fervor if we do not have a clear eschatological faith.

Another example of this is found in the words of a second chorus we use extensively.

"Let us fill the world with joy,
Let us fight and never faint,
Let us talk of Christ every day
And with Jesus transform all the world."

Here the element of perseverance is placed above the call, but the most significant thing is the believer's reorientation toward Jesus and His power. With Him we can transform the world! This was real to the early Christians and it is real for modern-day Christians who put their confidence in the risen Lord Who can take any kind of dead bones and revive them.

Actually, we use music to broaden the believer's perspective, to reprogram him and stimulate him to return to his first love, which is the key to all the evangelistic task.

Let me share one more chorus, in order to complete the full picture. The words go something like this:

"I am a messenger of the great King.
I will take His message of love
To the lost who have no salvation.
Lord, I will go, Lord, I will go."

Here we emphasize the need of obedience, followed by the understanding that it is not only the professional communicator who is privileged to take the good news to the lost, but also the common believer who received his training and practice immediately after his conversion, the believer who turned his spiritual experience into a romantic and pleasant reality, because every believer is a complete, present, and unlimited possibility in the hands of God when he shares what God has done for him.

So therefore it is highly important to include music in our seminars, by means of which we invite the participant to:
    a)   seek true communion with God
    b)   have the Lord in mind in every daily activity

c)   recognize that without God he can do nothing
d)   understand that the closer he gets to the light, the darker will
        his sins appear
e)   think that the love of God can only be proved if he loves his
        neighbor
f)   give thanks to God for what He has done, what He is doing,
        and what He will yet do in his life
g)   realize that his model is no human leader, even though he be
        someone good and honorable, but his model must be Jesus
        Christ, the Lamb of God
h)   shine for Christ in a natural way wherever he may be, with
        his own light, rather than waiting for ideal situations
i)   center his action in the irrefutable fact of the cross
j)   ask God to use him for His glory, every day
k)   render his life, his reason, and his body to God on a daily basis,
        as an absolute requirement for being perfectly synchronized
        with God and thus not give an uncertain sound when sharing
        the Gospel with the unconverted.

Chapter 27

Local Leaders Know Best

Seventh: Continuing with the series we were following previously, the seventh thing we hoped to do was sensitize the community regarding the evangelicals' power and strength, and as a result, project a new image of these Bible-centered people. This was amply achieved back in 1960 in Nicaragua, where even the non-Christians sang our theme choruses.

When we began Evangelism in Depth there, the Somoza family was in power with Luis, son of General Anastacio Somoza Debayle, in the presidency. The political situation was unstable. All entries and exits from Managua were manned by checkpoints and there was political repression as well as a defeatist attitude, evident in all the people including evangelicals.

I still recall the day of our final parade in Managua. We requested permission to march along a main avenue in front of the federal government building. Don Gilberto Aguirre, a great Christian layman, was driving his Landrover jeep and several of us rode in it at the head of the parade. Before starting out, we prayed and also asked ourselves what we would do it the soldiers started shooting.

Behind us was a truck full of leaders who were standing up, including Dr. Kenneth Strachan and a young lawyer named Rene Garcia. Following them, the people marched on foot singing "Nicaragua will be for the Saviour, if united we battle for Him." They sang with such conviction and enthusiasm that I'm sure the guardian angels' wings fluttered due to the decibels produced by a people willing to confess their faith.

Of course the year had not been easy. For example, in one region predominantly inhabited by the Molimbo Indians, by means of radio harangues the Catholic priests had succeeded in getting them to rise up and attack us. In Masaya, during a campaign held in front of the railroad station, a Catholic priest deliberately drove his jeep across twice between the crowd and the station platform while the service was in progress.

Nevertheless, the impact of a consecrated minority had been felt. Don Luis Somoza gave us an interview and permitted a young Colombian evangelist, Victor Garrido, to do a chalk drawing for him in the presidential palace. We were also given time on television.

Eighth: We wanted to structure a program of total mobilization, taking into consideration local needs and resources, on the individual as well as the institutional level, with the following indispensable factors:

a) drawing close to the Lord
b) becoming conscious of the responsibility to fulfil the Great Commission
c) putting into practice the ideas of local leaders

This latter point included our Evangelism in Depth offices. I remember that Mrs. Dolores Martinez, our secretary, had a typewriter that was at least 20 years old. As national coordinator, my desk consisted of an unpainted table and chair bought at the market. In front of the office, which was a house someone had loaned us for the year, we strung up a canvas sign proclaiming "National Office of Evangelism in Depth." We also had regional offices all over the country.

Don Kenneth, who lived in Costa Rica but visited regularly, was often frustrated with us, including my style of dress. I always wore a guayabera (tropical style shirt worn loosely). One day I suppose he could stand it no longer and he arrived in sweltering Managua with a blue suit for me.

I also recall how embarrassed he was to bring dignitaries to visit our offices, including Eric Fife, of InterVarsity Christian Fellowship; Jacob Stam, president of the L.A.M. board; the secretary for Latin America of the United Bible Societies, and others. It looked like anything but a place where a new chapter was being written in the continent's evangelical history.

Ninth: We wanted to teach all the Christians that God really gives them the ability to handle eternal truths adequately, adjusted to the needs of the receiver, from the very moment of their conversion. This philosophy of evangelism has persisted through all these years.

This spirit has not been vanquished, in spite of the fact that ideological enemies of Evangelism in Depth later took over its leadership for a short time in Costa Rica after I left the team. The situation became so difficult that even the name of Evangelism in Depth was buried in many parts of Latin America. Criticisms became sharper, to the point that to my sorrow even the EID director wrote something against total mobilization. In those days they considered Evangelism in Depth to be a failure, while I felt each movement was an interesting experiment (and there was always a great deal of fruit by way of souls saved).

The battle has been both internal and external, but like the rock of Gibraltar, EID has remained unaffected by the attacks of those who confused it with a program and could not, or would not, fully investigate this renovating action of the evangelical community. In fact there were certain companions who for years refused to publish anything about what was happening, even when at one time we had more than 7,000 churches cooperating.

Tenth: It was also necessary to ferret out the natural resources of the church, such as:

   a)   personnel capable of challenging God to fulfill His word
   b)   financial resources, both active and passive
   c)   local pastors with the ability to analyze and solve the different problems related to evangelism. One of these model pastors was Efrain Zarate of the Bible Society, a Guatemalan who had given his life and heart to Nicaragua.

To give impulse to national hymnology; to harmonize relationships between foreign missionary institutions with the national church in order to make an impact on the community; to seek a program that would really combine a genuine concern for reaching the lost with an absolute confidence in the Lord, as well as the theory and practice of communion with God and immediate evangelistic action, were other goals that we needed to take into account.

My wife, Elisabeth, registered many of these things in the book titled *Evangelism in Depth,* which was published by Moody Press, at that time led by Dr. Kenneth Taylor, prophet from the beginning of Evangelism in Depth.

For the reasons presented above, most of the programs ended up blending theory and practice with a dependence upon God through the prayer cells and through understanding that all people need to hear the Gospel, we all have the ability to testify, and therefore we can all do it. If we do not want to, well, that's something else. We are all obligated to proclaim the Gospel because all peoples have the sacred right to hear it.

Evangelism in Depth is not some imposed attitude. It is an urgent call to all Christians so that with a broad sense of responsibility, we may use all the resources at our command to allow the people who have not been born again to turn from the power of darkness to the living God, our Lord Jesus Christ.

Therefore we recommend that God's servants become involved in this ideology. Taking this concept of total mobilization into account, they should put all their own ideas (and those of others) into practice. Of course, no matter how brilliant an idea may be, if it does not produce born-again people it should be abandoned. On the other hand, every idea that results in new babes in Christ should be used and perfected until it no longer gives fruit.

Chapter 28

Bethel Church

It takes more work to carry out Evangelism in Depth, and in the beginning it produces fewer visible results, but in the end it is all worthwhile because its fruits are so deep and long lasting.

A clear example of this is Bethel Church, today a denomination with 200 churches. Eighteen years ago its pastor, the Rev. Ruben Ramirez, participated as one of Evangelism in Depth's vice presidents in Mexico. He says that in those days he had "seven churches, seven buildings, and seven pastors;" the central church in the city of Veracruz had a congregation of 200 people and the building measured 25 by 60 feet.

Up to now, he testifies, he has never stopped practicing Evangelism in Depth, which he credits with the church's amazing growth. Instead of seven churches at the beginning of EID in 1970, there are now 200. The central church holds 5,000 people. And pastor Ramirez says, "Every month we build a new church edifice." At this rate he may soon make it every week or every day! Why not?

Evangelism in Depth in Mexico was the broadest experiment ever in the history of EID. At that time, according to the Rev. Regino Palazuelos, who was national coordinator, "We were working with more than 9,000 churches from more than 47 denomination. 1972 was the beginning of a new era in the Mexican evangelical church, not only in regard to evangelism and the fruit of that evangelism, but also in regard to relationships among the different parts of the body of Christ."

Nevertheless, it is also good to recall that EID has some pitfalls that must be avoided if we hope to garner greater harvests. Since most churches are accustomed to holding campaigns, it is possible that very soon they just want to have campaigns. A campaign is wonderful; I am an evangelist and do all I possibly can to promote campaigns and participate in them; but EID is not a campaign. What is required is that every believer exercise his natural ability to talk to others about Christ.

This is total mobilization, which makes every believer an evangelizer, not an evangelist. Please understand that we are not against the great expositors of the salvation message. Far from it! But what we are doing is to emphasize the need of inverting our systems and methods of work into those that the New Testament clearly teaches.

Chapter 29

Presuppositions

Many people who criticize campaigns point out that they can cost a great deal of money and produce few results, that a campaign is an event and not a process, that the people who make decisions sometimes cannot be located afterward, and so forth. I would like to make my position clear in this regard.

Those who complain about campaigns are usually those who are not willing to work hard in the church, and who do not give first place to evangelism. They are the ones who do not raise a finger to make things turn out better, who do not understand that the evangelist is simply an instrument of God to explain the message. It is the pastor who must orient, guide, and motivate the flock.

When traditional campaigns fail it is usually because of the pastor's irresponsibility, rather than the evangelist's methods. Many of those who object to this method are not convinced that evangelism is the principle reason for the church's existence. In other words, we must avoid falling into the error of a destructive critical spirit that puts down evangelism by means of campaigns. God continues to use many of His servants in this field.

Nevertheless, it is even more exciting to think that God can use all of us as effective communicators of the good news of salvation. And therein lies the difference!

Once we understand the biblical foundation of total mobilization, meaning that we grasp the fact that Christ never taught His disciples a certain method nor did His disciples (rather, we must clearly see that all of us, if we are willing, can verbalize what God has done for us), then we must begin to plan a program that meets the needs and uses the resources of the area where this mobilization is to be implemented.

In order to do this, we should consider four presuppositions and four principles. Let us begin with the first presupposition.

1) An abundant harvest requires abundant planting.

I confess that although I did not comprehend what was behind all that my pastor led me to do when I was a new convert, yet I clearly realized that when young people participate in church and everyone works hard, there are results. Years later I realized I was part of a group that was planting abundantly.

Back in 1947 in Mexico City we initiated Youth for Christ. Bethlehem Presbyterian Church, where I attended, was a strong center of that activity, and I remember we evangelized in many ways. Early in the morning the pastor took us out to play basketball and then we shared the Gospel with our opponents. We organized rallies in the streets. We climbed into buses and, while part of the group played guitars and sang, the rest of us gave out tracts. We traveled on trains and held services from car to car.

Each Saturday night we had big youth rallies in different large churches such as First Baptist, Divine Saviour Presbyterian, Nazarene, Messiah Methodist, Christian and Missionary Alliance, Assemblies of God, Universal Christian, Salvation Army and so on. We worked hard, but we reaped abundantly. From our church alone, that year fourteen young people decided to dedicate their lives to serving the Lord.

In 1950 I was busy doing similar ministry in Central America when I had the opportunity of meeting Kenneth Strachan and he invited me to join the campaign department of the Latin America Mission with headquarters in San Jose, Costa Rica. At that time our total mobilization of young people in Guatemala was getting unprecedented results.

Since the time of Christ, His disciples have heard, "Open your eyes and look at the fields! They are ripe for harvest" . . . "Ask the Lord of the harvest, therefore, to send out workers into his harvest field" (John 4:35b, Luke 10:2b).

In reality one cannot say that people are not ready. The problem is that the church, in corporate or individual form, is not willing to take the message to them. There has never been a person who genuinely wanted to share the Gospel, who Christ has not honored with fruits. There has never been a time when people have not been ready to listen. But yes, there have been times when the church has refused to carry out its priority task.

The church's disobedience regarding evangelism is the reproach given in chapter 3 of the Revelation to Philadelphia. Our refusal to obey the Great Commission is what has marked periods of history in which the evangelistic flame has appeared to die out.

But wherever we go we find people thirsty for eternal truth. Children, young people, and adults demand the right to hear the message of redemption, but they also need to hear it in an intelligible, understandable way. We must never alter the content of the message, but we can vary the way of presentation, above all when we follow the Holy Spirit's guidance (as discussed previously).

Many believers try to rationalize their disobedience by quoting the passage where Jesus says, "A prophet is not without honor except in his own country and in his own house" (Matthew 13:57b NKJV). They say there is no prophet in his own country.

But they are misquoting. Christ points out that yes, there will be prophets in their own places, but they will not receive all the honor they deserve. And that, my friend, is very true!

But the other side of the coin is also true. In no other place can we be used as well as in our local area. There, with our friends, neighbors, relatives, fellow workers, and town leaders, we need no specialized preparation because we are at home. We need no extra time to witness because we are with these people all the time. We do not have to tear down walls because we know how those walls were built in the first place. We need no special funds, no different language. All we need to do is get on with the job.

Everything comes down to disobedience. I realize sometimes we feel embarrassed because we are unaware of the great resources God has given us in His word. Clearly, when carrying out a denominational, regional, statewide, or nationwide effort, we must sow much prayer, much work, much faith. But one of the beautiful things about Evangelism in Depth is that we feel bolstered by the fact that "everyone is doing it," and so we are motivated to dive in and try.

Paul said, "He who sows sparingly will also reap sparingly, and he who sows bountifully will also reap bountifully" (II Corinthians 9:6 NKJV). The land may be fertile, the weather may be perfect, there may be abundant seed, the rain may fall just when we need it, we may have sufficient workers, they may be very capable, our funds may be unlimited. But if we never sow the seed, or if we just sow a little, we will not harvest very much. It's just that simple.

Chapter 30

Training Centers

Let's take the prayer cells, for example. They are designed to become Bible study groups, centers for leadership training, missionary groups, and eventually even organized churches. Group dynamics are the tonic of each of these prayer cells, although the participants may not understand it that way. Their faith becomes stronger when they see their prayers answered; their spiritual growth is accelerated, and so on. But if we do not form prayer cells, we will have fewer results.

The time, spiritual resources, money, and personal energy we invest will produce abundant fruit as a natural consequence. In Mexico I have seen the Baptist church, which Juan Leon pastors, grow 30 per cent a year. And I have seen the Jerusalem Missionary church of Tepeapulco, Hidalgo, open 100 new missions in one year. I have seen more than 20,000 conversions in one week in simultaneous campaigns, where all but 25 of the thousand preachers were laymen, according to pastor Lenin Izquierdo of the gulf Presbytery in Mexico.

I have seen the Bell Bible church of California grow so much that the members began to think about enlarging their sanctuary to provide for 500 people. When they began with the ideas of total mobilization, they had about 150 people, according to pastor Francisco Ramirez.

Do you see the point? These principles work, but we must sow in faith, not doubting. In faith, which is the assurance of things hoped for, the conviction of things not seen. In faith, hope, love. We must remember that the quality of the seed is guaranteed, and the earth is prepared to produce at least a 30 per cent yield. Are you convinced? The problem is simply — you and I.

A friend of mine used to quote Matthew 9:37 this way, "The harvest is plentiful, but the laborers are lazy." If we do not harvest abundantly, it is simply because of what we have or have not sown. Much prayer, much direction from God. Little prayer, more human wisdom. More dependence on God, more of His power. Less closeness to Him, more human effort. More faith, more miracles beginning with conversions. More faithfulness to the word, more glory for Christ.

All very logical, isn't it?

Chapter 31

No More Tourists!

Now let's think about the second presupposition.

2)   When Christians share their resources for evangelism, God multiplies them.

This has very practical applications. It means each passenger on the boat should have his own oar to row with, not like the tourist boat in Xochimilco where there are several kinds of vessels: those that move with an external power such as an outboard motor; those that are meant to carry tourists where the boatman does all the work while the guests simply sit back and enjoy the ride; and the racing boats where each person has an oar. When every believer participates in the evangelization of his community and his immediate vicinity, then there is multiplication of energies and of results.

When we come to the phase of visiting house to house in EID, for example, the possibility of visiting thousands of homes is greatly expanded. Suppose we hope to visit 100,000 homes, dedicating half an hour in each one. If the evangelism committee of the local church decides to do it, it will take forever. But if ten churches with 100 members in each one unite their resources, then the job becomes feasible. If each believer gives four hours a week to visitation, he'll visit eight homes a week, making a total of 800 for each church. It won't take long to reach all 100,000 at that rate.

Do you see? It's so easy to do the work when we join our resources together!

In one country when we carried out Evangelism in Depth, we printed many thousands of handbills on which each church could stamp its own address. The cost was infinitesimal in comparison to what it would have cost for each church to print their handbills separately.

Another example: in Mexico during 1971 and 1972 we published Evangelism in Depth's newspaper *En Marcha* in editions of 100,000 each, with all the cost paid by local organizations.

The same principle applies to the talents and gifts of the churches. God multiplies these resources for evangelism. He has not promised to help us build new educational plants (although He often does) but yes, He has pledged His word with regard to world evangelization. We can be sure of His guaranteed presence in such activities.

There is a third presupposition which is no less important than the first two:

3) Christians can and should work together in evangelism.

What do we mean by that? Well, it is neither possible nor necessary for us to be united in liturgy, doctrinal emphasis, organization or certain theological concepts. But in evangelism we are obliged to work together. This is Christ's clear mandate in John 17:21 where He says, "That all of them may be one, Father, just as you are in me and I am in you. May they also be in us so that the world may believe that you have sent me."

That is, the participation of all believers in evangelistic proclamation has saving effects, "that the world may believe."

Chapter **32**

They Are All My Children

Paul compares the Church to a body, and says that no organ can usurp the function of another. I understand this is the ministry of complementing each other. That is, no church as a member of the Body of Christ is complete without the participation of the rest.

I remember one pastoral retreat. When it came time to pray, there was a small group of three: a Presbyterian, a Baptist, and a Pentecostal. The Pentecostal pastor opened his lungs and cried out to God with his requests. When he finished the other two asked him reproachfully, "Brother, why do you shout? Do you think God is deaf?"

The pastor begged their pardon and commented, "Brethren, that's just the way we are. I didn't intend to offend you. I believe you are right; God is not deaf."

But the next day he said to the Baptist and the Presbyterian, "I've been thinking about what you said yesterday. You're right, God is not deaf, but I would like to point out that my loud volume does not bother Him, because He's not nervous either."

How true! God accepts us as we are. Undoubtedly, He wants us to worship Him with all our heart, with absolute sincerity, but the bottom line is that we do worship, even if we do so childishly, stuttering, or so overcome with emotion that all our body trembles. The important thing to Him is that we spend time in prayer. He arranges everything so our stumbling efforts turn into praise for His glory.

I have four children, all of them in God's service in one way or another, for which I never cease to praise Him. But they are all different. One of my daughters is extremely intelligent. Like her mother, she can think of five things at the same time. I suppose she is bored by a conversation on a single channel.

Another of my daughters is very sensitive; she is like one of our granddaughters who is named Cynthia. All we need to do is give her an angry look and she begins to cry as though the world were coming to an end. So I have to be very careful not to offend or hurt my daughter.

When my third daughter was a child, she was a literalist. If I said, "Please pass the salt," she would grasp the salt shaker, pass it through the air in front of my nose, and set it down again on the table. I almost had to say, "Daughter, in front of you is a curved object containing salt. Please reach out your arm, open your hand to pick up the object, hold it firmly between your thumb and index finger, lift it in the air, transport it to your right about a yard, lower your arm, and free the object, placing it on the table in front of me."

Ridiculous? Of course. But she played with us that way and forced us to be precise. We all laughed while we learned the lesson.

But I cannot deny that she is my daughter. They all are! And that's the way with the family of God. We are all so different!

If someone teaches that Jesus Christ is the only mediator between God and man, that Jesus Christ died for our sins on the cross of Calvary, that man by nature is a sinner, that the Bible is the Word of God . . . if someone teaches these things, then he is my brother in Christ. He is born again. He is a child of God just as much as I am. He has been bought with the same price, not with silver or gold, but with the precious blood of Christ. He has the same master.

Then what is the problem? In Evangelism in Depth no one puts his particular convictions aside. On the contrary, he believes them more firmly than ever. But he becomes aware that other believers are also part of God's family. We do not promote a super organization but rather a spirit of cooperation, by means of which we give testimony so that the world may believe. After all, if we are to be together in heaven, it's good to get accustomed to being together down here. We can get practiced up!

Now we come to the last of the presuppositions. It is just as important as the others:

4) A consecrated minority can make an impact on an entire nation.

Many times we have seen this come true. During more than a fourth of a century I have dedicated my life to evangelism. In 1953 Kenneth Strachan said I was the only Latin in full-time evangelism in Latin America. I am not sure that was true, but he said it.

At any rate, one example of the truth of this presupposition happened in Paraguay. On a certain Sunday night we began a campaign in the Communeros Stadium of Asuncion, but when we returned for the Monday night meeting, the stadium was closed. Who could help us reach the president in order to get permission to continue our campaign? It was not achieved through some highly-placed religious personality, nor an important politician, but through a humble Christian who happened to be General Stroesner's personal barber. A consecrated minority can make an impact on an entire nation!

In Costa Rica we had a permit from the governor of San Jose province to finish our evangelistic activity with a parade. During Evangelism in Depth we had the privilege of airing the first evangelical television program in Costa Rica, called "Moments of Inspiration." We were also the first group to cooperate with funds so that the government could roof over the national stadium. Nevertheless, at the last minute before the parade, President Mario Echandi intervened to cancel our permit. Once again it was a small minority that managed to rescind his order. Led by an evangelical engineer, Enrique Cabezas, who at the time was president of the Evangelical Alliance, we visited newspapers, radio stations, judicial authorities, and . . . believe it or not, we won the injunction against the president. Of course it is important to point out that in Costa Rica, democracy is a fact, not just an illusion.

In Peru, although the streets were full of tanks and soldiers because of civil unrest, the evangelicals paraded to the center of Lima to sing "A Mighty Fortress Is Our God" and "Peru will be for the Saviour, if united we battle for Him."

In Mexico, on March 21, 1972, the general director of the Federal District's government ordered us to suspend an activity we had planned: to pay homage to Mexico's great reformer Benito Juarez; it was to have been the culmination of the first phase of Evangelism in Depth.

At that time, the reverend Rafael Ayala, a unique friend, said to the government, "It would be a great honor to be punished for paying homage to the person who passed the law giving Mexico freedom of religion." And that afternoon 60,000 people marched from the Monument to the Revolution down the avenues to Alameda Park where the imposing Juarez monument stands. The lawyer who had tried to stop us, finally appeared at the closing ceremony.

All six lanes of Juarez avenue were closed to traffic in front of the Juarez monument for several hours that afternoon so that we 60,000 evangelicals (some reported more, some less) could carry out our program in a city which at that time had some 11,000,000 inhabitants.

In the Dominican Republic, as I mentioned, civil war broke out the very night the evangelical leaders had set aside for an all-night prayer meeting to initiate Evangelism in Depth and place it in God's hands. While we were on our knees before the Lord, we could hear the rumbling of tanks.

During that EID effort, one of our companions, Mario, lost everything when his house was set on fire. William Cook was saved from a bombing one day because he arrived home five minutes late; fellow missionary Jim Cochrane had suggested he buy something to eat before going home, in case it were impossible to leave later. And then we heard that the Cook's rented home had been bombed. Someone had hit it with a shell which set the house afire.

Another team member, Candido, was at the point of losing his life when they shot at him, but fortunately the bullet passed a little high and hit the inside light of the car where he was sitting. Just a sliver grazed his forehead.

Brother Jim Cochrane took us in the night of April 13, when 700 people died in a cleanup operation, even though he was in danger of having his house confused with a commando hideout.

And lawyer Alfonso Lockward, president of EID in the Dominican Republic, founded a church in the rebel zone. Brave actions of small minorities!

I'd also like to mention that although the Constitution of Peru held that evangelicals were second class citizens, one prominent evangelical — lawyer Pedro Arana — was able to participate in a change in his country's Constitution which eliminated that clause. Of course it was God's doing, but he was the instrument.

Chapter 33

Help From Non-Christians

Perhaps nothing can compare with our experience in Guatemala. It was November 25, 1962. We had planned to hold a national rally of evangelical forces in the Mateo Flores stadium of Guatemala City, which would be the final act of a year-long movement of Evangelism in Depth, initiated the previous January with a pastoral retreat in the Industrial Park with some 1,500 in attendance.

That day we expected 75,000 people. What joyous anticipation! But early in the morning a military revolution exploded. A squadron of planes dropped bombs on the presidential mansion and the entire city was terrified. The buses and truckloads of people coming into Guatemala City from the countryside were turned back by police; none were allowed to enter!

The Evangelism in Depth executive committee held an emergency meeting. After considering reasons for and against, they decided to cancel the meeting and the parade which was to have started off from Bolivar Park. I was not present in the session when they made that decision; I was too busy with final preparations for the meeting, dealing with the authorities, and all the other problems that fell under my responsibility as national coordinator.

The committee came to advise me of their decision. The plan had been for the evangelical radio station to play the series of choruses the paraders would sing, so all the marchers could use the radio to coordinate the songs, but the station switched to a different kind of music.

Thanks to some information I brought, the committee met to reconsider, and finally said no again. Everything must be cancelled! The planes might come back and attack all the people in the parade, and so on . . . .

When Don Luis Perez realized the decision was irrevocable, because Dr. Strachan had favored the cancellation, he suggested we go to the park to see if anyone had arrived for the parade. He was EID treasurer. Several of us joined him and went to the park. I was certain many people would be there, but had no idea how many.

When we arrived, there must have been about 20,000 believers lined up with large posters, floats, flags with the words "Guatemala will be for the Saviour" and other slogans, decorated bicycles, cars, and so on.

As carefully as possible the committee tried to explain the dangers to the crowd and their decision to cancel.

The president of the EID committee was not with us. But at that strategic moment a humble Indian believer, probably from the country around Lake Atitlan, said something like this, "Brother, if you are afraid, go back home. We are going to march."

With that spark, the fire was ablaze. Every denomination had its own float and signs and the plan was for all their members to march together behind them. But with the hasty decision to go ahead, there was no time to lose. All the organizational details had to be passed over in the rush, and so the Presbyterians ended up behind the Pentecostal float, the Baptists behind the Nazarenes, and so forth. Not bad!

Chapter 34

President Ydigoras Fuentes

When we arrived at the stadium we were a united people with the desire to win Guatemala for Christ. Our Evangelism in Depth president, Dr. Virgil Zapata, had joined the parade at the Cinco Calles intersection. The final meeting got underway, with the 500-voice choir singing under the enthusiastic direction of Oscar Lopez, now Dr. Lopez, and I was in charge of the congregational singing.

In the midst of that glorious hymn "How Great Thou Art," the stadium doors suddenly opened and several jeeps entered with armed soldiers. The crowd was alarmed, but then they recognized a famous figure descending from a vehicle with a machine gun slung over his shoulder, shirt collar unbuttoned, followed by a group of other special people: the president of the Senate, of the Congress, and of the Supreme Court, plus other officials and guards, all accompanying the president of the republic.

Without much fanfare they took their places near the pulpit and listened to the message given that afternoon by evangelist Fernando Vangioni. The very day their enemies had attempted to kill them or at least put them out of office!

Among the visitors in Guatemala that weekend to observe Evangelism in Depth's finale were some pastors from the U.S.A. and a group of laymen from their churches, including Spencer Bower, beloved Christian statesman, who since that day has been a firm backer of EID. It was he who had faith in the ideas presented in my book *The Other Side of the Coin* a year later.

As the president listened respectfully to the program, one of our foreign visitors decided to take a photo of him. Another of the tourists egged him on saying, "Shoot him! Shoot!" It was meant innocently enough, and the visitors assumed no one of the president's party understood English, but one of the bodyguards leaned over and admonished with a perfect American accent, "Don't say shoot; just take the picture." An unforgettable memory!

According to many comments heard later, the evangelicals saved Guatemala from a military coup that day without intending to. Yes, a consecrated minority can make an impact on an entire country, according to the fourth presupposition of Evangelism in Depth. I can think of no better example.

Paraphrasing Paul: And what more shall I say? For time would fail me to tell of Colombia, Ecuador, Honduras, Bolivia, and Venezuela. In each of these places it was made evident that a consecrated minority could make an impact on the entire nation. The evangelicals, united and inspired by John 17:21, proved again and again that Christians can work together in evangelism, because he who sows abundantly will also reap abundantly.

Now we come to what we call the principles. Four principles implied in the following statement: **Total mobilization of Christians to give testimony of their faith, within the frame of reference of the local church, by means of local leadership and with global objectives.**
What do we mean by all that? Many interesting things.
If we accept the fact that all believers are capable of witnessing successfully at the very moment of their conversion, it should not be difficult for us to organize and motivate them so they all do it. Of course we are not thinking only of the members of a local church body; at a given time many churches can be organized on a denominational, regional, or statewide level.
This obviously includes all the evangelical family, whether or not all are members of a church. Their official affiliation gives them the right to vote and enjoy certain privileges in their local congregation, but as soon as they are converted they should immediately go into action in evangelism, just as the ex-madman of the Gadarenes.
God's come and go are tightly intertwined. Neither time nor space can separate them. We are all capable of witnessing with all the power of God and in all places. We must remember that this lifestyle was practiced by the Lord Jesus Christ and if He did it as our example, I believe we are to follow in His steps and obey His commands.
When we say that this mobilization should be done within the context of the local church, we refer to several things. First, we make it clear that the local church, as an institution with all its defects, is the visible witness left by the Lord on earth. The church as an organism or as an expression on the local level is the beginning point. It should be, for evangelistic activity. Those who look down on the church are in error, and their legacy may be many spiritual children who will not have proper doctrinal food for their appropriate growth in Christ.
The church is the place where the ministry of follow-up and consolidation can be exercised properly. I firmly believe that the follow-up of the new believer occurs in four phases.
The first is when someone witnessed to the person, who then accepts Christ.
The second phase occurs when he receives an elementary doctrinal

explanation, sufficient to help him understand his new relationship with God biblically. By means of the first programed lessons, the new believer acquires an older brother who takes the place of Ananias in the case of Paul. The discipler and the evangelizer may, of course, be the same individual.

The third phase has to do with the officials of the local church, who will teach him practical ecclesiology such as how to pray, why we do not have images in our places of worship, how to find Bible passages, what is the pastor's function, why we take offerings, what activities he may participate in, and so on. In other words, the new believer is integrated into the liturgy and style of the congregation to which he will relate as he grows into spiritual maturity.

I confess that it bothers me to arrive at a church where no one greets me or hands me a hymnal (in Latin America, few churches provide Bibles or hymnals in the pews). It seems shameful not to welcome visitors. The church should be like a home; members and visitors alike should feel content, leaving with a strong desire to conquer the world for Christ and live a victorious life according to Scriptural principles. An abundant life! But if he feels unwelcome, unnoticed, ignored, his response will be frustration and defeat.

The fourth phase which completes the follow-up of the new believer, occurs when he is integrated into the framework of the denomination or movement to which the church belongs. He comes to understand why his last name is Baptist, Pentecostal, Presbyterian, etcetera.

Now we come to the third principle, which involves a depth that we should not treat lightly, even though it appears to be a simple idea, because to do so would be to ignore the very nerve center of total mobilization. It says merely "by means of local leadership."

Too long the importance of local leadership has been passed over by evangelical organizations. This may appear difficult to accept, but it's a fact. It's true that each believer has his own social universe in which he is the center, but it is also true that within a region or country there are numerous variables, even on a state level or within a capital city. The way things are done in one part of the city may be different from another part, simply because of the type of people who live in each place.

Using local leadership presupposes consulting them, dialoguing with them, making agreements with them, including them in decisions, respecting their way of doing things, understanding their value systems, their vocabulary, their surroundings. It is only when we take them into account that we can say we are working with any sense of permanence.

As a matter of record, most church organizations are unable to identify with the various social levels and problems where they are located. So it is indispensable to consider local leadership as a determining factor for doing an adequate job of total mobilization.

Furthermore, we must consider the value of the present in the local church. We need to know the spiritual state of the people, at least on a partial level. The movement of God's Spirit can sometimes be felt in a still small voice instead of a great and strong wind that breaks the rocks in pieces. I realize that in the Latin American context, local leaders are often close to being spiritual bosses, but that does not change the fact that they are the key figures in their churches, regardless of their idiosyncrasies.

Many churches seem to be perpetually dependent on the outside, which is not always healthy and can be a problem for new leaders who come in. In our Latin America, the man who wants to do something big in Christian work has to seek out the local leaders and get to know them, but not try to manipulate them, if he hopes to be successful in extending the Kingdom of God.

We have now arrived at the last of EID's basic principles. Just to review, our statement in its entirety reads, "Total mobilization of Christians to give testimony to their faith, within the frame of reference of the local church, by means of local leadership and with global objectives."

Global objectives. This is perhaps the most difficult, because we are accustomed to living in Jerusalem, Judea, and Samaria, but very few of us have "to the uttermost part of the earth" in mind. This geographic dimension is very important.

What few people realize is that we should have a very broad criteria in evangelism. We should have strategies to reach all the police force, all the newsmen, all the military, all the politicians, all the businessmen, all the schools, all the taxi drivers, all the prisoners, all the hospitals, all the sections of the city, everyone! See what I mean?

The church should not operate with nearsighted vision. The church should see an opportunity and a challenge in every segment of the nation. A challenge to think big, and an opportunity to see the works of God manifest.

Chapter 35

Back to Our First Love

 The challenge is to act like a people who are more than conquerors. The opportunity is to see how many things can be accomplished when we depend on God and work together in evangelism with the faith, security, and enthusiasm of our first love.

Not in vain did Jesus leave us His words, even though spoken at the last minute, as presented by the Gospel writers, with these orders: "Go therefore and make disciples of all nations, baptizing them in the name of the Father and of the Son and of the Holy Spirit, teaching them to observe all that I have commanded you; and lo, I am with you always, even to the end of the age" (Matthew 28:19,20).

In other words, to all the world, with all the power, all the days, all the things, all His presence, all the time, all the believers with all the faith that is the assurance of things hoped for, the conviction of things not seen, although the quality of the communication of the Gospel of salvation will always be a prerogative of the Holy Spirit.

That's why the second verse of the song, "Our Country Will Be For The Saviour" goes like this:

"From the north to the south and all over,
East and west need to hear about Him,
It's the message that offers redemption
From sin to a new life in Him.
In every town, every house, every city
We must preach about Christ everywhere.
Yes, they all need to know He can save them from sin
And soon He'll come again!"

That's why we should "Go into all the world," including our world, and that of others. And if we remember that the Lord has promised to be with us always, until the end of the world, then total mobilization and evangelizing in depth will be so easy, so very easy, that not to do it is sin.

The other evangelism, the kind that Jesus did, is what we need to transform the world. Evangelism in Depth is nothing new; it all comes from the book of Acts. A return to our first love is the only answer.

The Church needs to hear again the voice of the Lord saying, "But I have this against you, that you have abandoned the love you had at first" (Revelation 2:4). Biblically speaking, we can never give witness by merely living a Christian life without speaking.

We must speak, because Christ said, "I tell you, if these were silent, the very stones would cry out" (Luke 19:40). God has given us the privilege of being firsthand witnesses. Let us be faithful ones, so that the Kingdom of God and of His Christ may come at last on the earth and we may take part in the great supper of the Lamb, where we will sing, "You are worthy, our Lord and God, to receive glory and honor and power, for you created all things, and by your will they were created and have their being" (Revelation 4:11).

Our methods in the future should begin with the fact that even though we Latin Americans all speak the same language, we are as different as the moon and the stars in our way of doing things, and the same is true in other parts of the world. We all shine, thanks to the Son of Justice that illuminates us, but we all need our own sky. Otherwise, we will not have correct answers for real needs. We require more dependence on God, obviously, but we also need more dependence on one another in a practical way.

A Biblical basis without a strategy and methodology adjusted to regional idiosyncrasies, produces an evangelistic ministry which is slow and often ineffective from the human point of view. Imagination and creativity without an adequate Biblical foundation is fertile ground for far-out evangelical groups that easily fall prey to the false sects with Christian names.

Success in evangelism resides in the practice of all the methods that God has specifically approved in the book of Acts. The practice of all of them in the church and by the church, will give us an effective, contemporary, and Biblical methodology. Outside of this scriptural context, all the rest are mere intents at evangelization.

Evangelization requires teaching all the counsel of God, which will provide opportunity for God's creativity, expressed through His children, with new methods every single morning, every single hour, because, as we have explained, the believer is a present, permanent and complete possibility in God's hands when in the fervor of his first love.

With that spiritual understanding, evangelism (sharing our faith in our own way) becomes a romance that provides unspeakable joy all the time. The clear idea of God's "come and go" is a must for every Christian if we want to see the world reached for Christ.

What Is Evangelism in Depth in Practical Terms?

* It is each Christian taking Jesus' words in Luke 14:26,27 seriously, deciding to be a true disciple.
* It is each pastor teaching his church the principles of total mobilization, instead of thinking he is the only person responsible for evangelizing others.
* It is every Christian sharing the great news of salvation with all his or her contacts, backing up his words with a holy and consecrated life.
* It is every church losing the fear of opening its doors to people of the community and seeking ways to reach them with the Gospel.
* It is every believer renewing his or her first love for Jesus Christ (Revelation 2:4).
* It is every child of God doing the good works which God prepared beforehand, that he should walk in them (Ephesians 2:10).
* It is every Christian family demonstrating God's love through the atmosphere of the home and relationships with each member of the family, in order to prove the reality of the power of the Lord in their daily lives and thus have moral authority to back up the salvation message with practical demonstrations.
* It is every Christian home being conscious of its duty to be a center for prayer, Bible study, and testimony.
* It is the Church in general, shining with the light of the Gospel and the peace and holiness of its life before all the community which surrounds and observes it.
* It is every redeemed individual, putting the Lord's work in first place in thought, action, and pocketbook, willing to give for the cause of Christ ahead of satisfying his or her own desires.
* It is the Holy Spirit working through the children of God to prove that Christian love is something real, something true, according to the norms presented in I John 3:16-18.
* It is all the Body of Christ fulfilling the missionary purpose of God, by all possible means, trusting in Him who will have the final victory and Who does not want any to perish.

What Do People Say About Evangelism in Depth?

(some opinions about long-term EID movement or brief seminars)

From the U.S.A.

The Rev. Ron Thompson, Executive Director, Brethren Evangelistic Ministries, 1988:
"No doubt about it, First Love Renewal is a help to the churches. In the words of Scripture, it's now like a cloud about the size of a man's hand, but I see it growing. I see the blessing and those who have attended and who have felt the Spirit of God in their hearts and have been released from their fear and guilt to share their faith, have said with almost universal praise, it's one of the greatest things that's ever happened in their lives. It's brought us back to our first love and we praise the Lord for that."

The Rev. Don Rough, pastor, Riverside Grace Brethren Church, Johnstown, Pennsylvania, 1988:
"Our people are excited. They are looking forward to great things with God. It is interesting to see how God prepared the people for this past weekend (First Love Renewal seminar on Evangelism in Depth) and now it will be interesting to see how God works in the future. I definitely agree with the teaching; it's right there in Scripture. I'll try to follow up on the teaching. Yes, I would recommend these seminars. For one reason, what the Scripture says about sharing our faith. And the other reason would be because of the renewal itself, what it does and what it's like. It takes us back to our love for the Lord; the music, the singing, the preaching, and the teaching all go together and I just thank the Lord for it."

Evangelist Alan Read, Calvary Baptist Church, Danville, Illinois, 1988:
"This is exactly what we need, in the sense that it brings us back to the balance of outreach and being concerned about what Christ was concerned for . . . . The churches of America have prided themselves on building buildings and coming up with innovative programs and methods to reach people and we've strapped ourselves too much. We've lost sight of the reality of God's power . . . to have the presence and love of Christ

in the life so it just bubbles over in every area, in every conversation. This whole concept of First Love Renewal in the hearts of God's people causes others to pick up on it and desire it in their lives. This type of saturation evangelization is so important.

"These seminars liberate people from thinking they have to be professional, or have a special gift, or have a unique vision or calling from God. The fact that every born again Christian has the capacity to share that love for Christ is so desperately needed in a country where we have become so profession oriented, so career oriented . . . Christ can overcome these hurdles and show us a new philosophy and outlook that is very biblical.

"Of course that is the key. This is something right out of the Word of God. It's not man's invention and so I hope God is really going to bless it. In fact, He has already blessed it. This is the third seminar I've been in and by far the best one we've seen yet. There were actually people saved this weekend as a result of just everyday normal people out there in the pew telling their friends about the Lord Jesus."

Dr. Luis Palau, internationally known evangelist, 1988:
"I would recommend Evangelism in Depth, in the first place because of its origin. I did not take part in its beginnings but I was blessed by it in the 1960's, and I believe Evangelism in Depth was born in the heart of God and for that reason I recommend it.

"Secondly, I would recommend EID because our continent needs it. It needs cooperation from Christians, the use of the gifts of the Spirit, the vision of an entire country and not merely a region, a town, or a city. It is a totally biblical vision."

Dr. Kenneth Taylor, paraphraser of The Living Bible, observer of the first Evangelism in Depth experiment in Nicaragua in 1960:
"Do you think that what is going on in Nicaragua may be of such importance that it should be widely publicized? It seems to me that missions and church groups in other parts of Latin America and throughout the world should be alerted, in the hope that they will do likewise in their own nations . . . .

"The aspect of the Nicaraguan situation that is so fascinating to me is that it has shortcut the Gordian knot of cooperation between various churches and missions . . . Is not this more and more what is needed abroad? Not that missionaries will be depended on to do the witnessing, but to help release the enormous Holy Spirit energy that is in every Christian congregation everywhere throughout the world? This, of course, is no new idea, because it has been quietly and increasingly developing for many years; perhaps all that I am doing is giving myself a reminder of the utter logic of what is going on in Nicaragua at the present time and what I think should soon go on in several other countries."

Various laymen who attended EID seminar in Community Grace Brethren Church, Long Beach, California, 1987:
"Most helpful and very biblical. The concentration of many Scriptures to teach the Bible truths has great impact. This seminar was of great value to me in many ways, the main way being that I have been praying that the Lord would renew my first love and heart for Jesus, Himself, that I might be focused on Him and be able to share Him with others in a natural way . . . God has used it to revive, challenge, and bless our hearts."

"Terrific! It has changed my life! Every Christian should hear it."

"Simplistic good stuff. Showing love of Christ is basic for all! Gives more confidence in the Holy Spirit and shows we are all needed in the body. No method in particular, just tell them what He has done for you!"

"It was very good . . . enjoyable, fulfilling, needed throughout America and the world."

"Very beneficial and informative. I enjoyed the simplicity of the seminar. Removing my attitude of complacency and replacing it with motivation and encouragement."

"Informative, motivational, doctrine-filled to meet and answer any questions or doubts about accomplishing our Christian purpose and responsibilities. It has made me aware of how I have been living a safe life by associating with only saved Christians so as not to have to face ridicule or persecution. I now have the strength and ability to go out in the world with a different drive and perspective to seek out and look for opportunities to keep Christ alive to others, not just in actions and intentions but in words."

From Guatemala:

Pastor Juan Augusto Sanz Archila, of the Golden Candlestick Church in San Pedro Zacatepeque, San Marcos, Guatemala, 1986:
"Evangelism in Depth is still an inspiration for me. When it took place in Guatemala (1962) I was very young, about 15 years old, but I well remember the activities and a book that I obtained called *The Authentic Revolutionaries* . . . There has not been another movement similar to EID, with the same strategies. Evangelism in Depth practically holds the record that no other movement has surpassed. The church I pastor has 1,500 members and they are always singing some of your hymns, especially 'O Lord, accept me just as I am' which has been a great blessing and inspiration for our church and for each member. We also sing 'Guatemala will be for the Saviour.' It was as a result of Evangelism in Depth that God called me into the pastorate . . . then I went to the Central American Bible Institute and that's how I became involved in the work of the Lord."

Edmundo Madrid, coordinator of Evangelism in Depth in Zacapa, Guatemala, in 1962; when interviewed in 1987 he was president of the Guatemalan Evangelical Alliance:

"In my own formation my participation in Evangelism in Depth left an indelible mark. I would say that back then the things that seemed to me most effective, were that there was training for those who were to be counselors, and that we were to go house to house. It was done more meticulously than anything we have done since. The united choir that we formed was very practical . . . I myself became a choir director.

"But the effort to train a large number of believers for evangelism and follow-up has not been repeated since, or if we have done it, it has been more superficial. A movement and emphasis on training every one of the believers for his participation is needed.

"What I remember most was the choir and I still have the EID hymnal. The other thing was the house to house visitation with the evangelistic message that we had understood. As a pastor, we mobilized the entire church and now I am a pastor and I know that it is not easy to mobilize a large group to go systematically to knock on doors. Knocking on doors is not the whole answer, but it gives us a great opportunity to find needs that we do not even imagine when we simply stay inside the walls of our churches.

"Now that I am president of the Evangelical Alliance I find myself at this crossroads with the diversity of opinions and attitudes of the evangelical groups, and really it is not easy to harmonize criteria, attitudes, and ideals. But yes, I believe movements that go beyond the boundaries of one denomination tend to unify the people of God . . . when a denomination participates seriously only in its own local activities, its members become exclusivistic and do not want to relate to brethren of other groups and this is not a healthy attitude. Movements that transcend denominational boundaries among evangelicals are needed to destroy these walls and unite our people spiritually and emotionally."

From Africa:

Willys K. Braun, coordinator of the national office of evangelism of the Congo Republic, writing an article in 1968 titled "Christ Pour Tous" regarding New Life for All, the African version of EID:

"Nationalism is the most inescapable fact of contemporary Africa . . . In view of this concern with the nation, it was natural and easy for the leaders of the Congo church in 1966 to approve a proposed plan for carrying out a national campaign of evangelism of two years duration. The plan was a transplant of Evangelism in Depth in Latin America. We lacked the consecrated and experienced Latin America Mission team, and the adequate budget of Venezuela and Peru; but within these limitations the principles and practices of Evangelism in Depth were fol-

lowed — with a French accent — with impressive results . . . .
"Thousands of people were won to Christ, through these varied efforts, and the churches became happy and vigorous centers of light and salvation. Several denominations baptized more than 5,000 people each. Individual congregations grew to double their original size; some added as many as 800 members in one year. Sunday Schools memorized thousands of Bible verses and doubled or tripled their attendance.

"On top of all this activity at the local and denominational level, firm steps forward were taken toward an effective and continuous program of evangelism on a national scale. The national evangelism committee, named in 1966, prepared the national two year plan and organized thirteen provincial evangelism conferences in which delegates of all the denominations participated.

"A national evangelism office and a secretary of evangelism supported by the denominations is dedicated to the preparation of special literature for the programs of each month. In the immediate future it is planned to establish provincial evangelism offices. For the first time Congo has a national evangelist whose ministry has been powerfully blessed by God. More than 7,000 decisions for Christ were registered in his recent three week campaign in the northwest zone of the Congo . . . .

"This experience in Evangelism in Depth has done marvellous things for the Congo. In March, leaders of churches and missions unanimously voted to continue the program during a third year. But we are sure that when this year has officially ended, the true work of evangelism on a national scale will continue, and that more than a million men and women will be converted to Christ during the next ten years."

From the Dominican Republic:

Alejandro Paniagua, journalist, published this editorial comment on Evangelism in Depth in the Dominican Republic's *Listin Diario* in 1966:
"From their prayer rooms and humble pulpits, the Dominican evangelicals have begun to project themselves in society; to come out of their anonymity; to make themselves known in a big way; to make themselves felt; to enter into the conscience of this people . . . The religious happenings protagonized by them in the last few months make us recall the early days of the apostolic church: when they could not be ignored while they carried on a spiritual revolution which was to transform the world.

"Evangelicals sometimes give the impression of being people who are only concerned with the religious aspect and disparage work and concern for social happenings.

"In reality they have not been understood. Because they are hardworking studious people who occupy their free time in a strong program of ecclesiastical activities and healthy recreation, while others dedicate their time to enjoying themselves in other ways and do directly political labor.

"In the social aspect evangelicals are citizens who are concerned about national happenings with a very clear idea of political problems and a civic attitude which is consistent with social needs and changes.

"That is to say, the Gospel produces a citizen who is respectful of the law; a man who is interested in the progress of the country; an honest public official; a hardworking student and farmer; a progressive laborer; a serious employee.

"It produces people with a discipline of spiritual progress directed toward the destruction of hatred, of egoism, of envy, and of lustful financial ambition.

"People who are quick to unite with common interests, to promote altruism on behalf of the community and sacrifice for their fellow men.

"The Evangelism in Depth campaign has united 90 per cent of the 40,000 evangelicals of the country in the work of extensive and profound — in depth — divulgation of the doctrines of the Christian religion.

"And upon mobilizing their activistic nucleus it has demonstrated that in the Dominican Republic these people represent a force.

"A moral force that serves to support a dislocated, disoriented society which seeks an encounter with itself. As Jesus Christ said, they are 'the salt of the earth.'

"This is what the Dominican evangelicals are demonstrating.

"And now more than ever, they are projecting their message and their dynamics, with the desire of achieving transformations that will send the country along the path toward social and economic progress."

J. Allen Thompson, field director of West Indies Mission in the Dominican Republic, 1966, wrote in Whitened Harvest magazine:
"Twelve months ago hopes for triumph seemed scant. At the close of the first EID pastors' retreat at the WIM center in La Vega, chilling announcements of a bloody revolution's outbreak filled the air. These reports stated: 'A military coup has taken over the government! Shooting and bombing have broken out on the streets of Santo Domingo.'

"Revolution! Would this be the death knell to Gospel endeavor? Could our heart longings and prayers for revival be realized in a nation at civil war? On the other hand, has the Church of Jesus Christ nothing to offer to downtrodden people seeking solutions to dire living conditions, illiteracy, exploitation, poverty? Does the Gospel change only the soul of man, or can we see it revolutionizing the home, the job, the nation? The little band of workers — Dominican Christians, missionaries, and EID personnel — declared themselves in favor of identification for Christ's sake with the people and their problems. The ominous circumstances of the revolution would be utilized, not shunned. As one of the Latin leaders, Juan Isais, put it: 'This is the time to strike. The spirit of action in a revolution is the spirit of growth.'

"So, in stormy days and with the pounding of gunfire about them, soldiers of the Cross began to penetrate with the Gospel a country that was destined for spiritual renaissance . . . That this mission was accomplished during a bitter revolution demonstrates the spirit and responsibility of a revived Church."

From Bolivia:

A Christian woman in Guayaramarine, Bolivia, told the following to the Rev. Charles Koch in 1965:

"Evangelism in Depth has been a wonderful thing for me and for our church. Before, we thought that the job of witnessing was in the hands of our pastor. My husband was converted a short time ago, although I have been a Christian for quite a while . . . .

"We listen to the radio program, 'Llamada a la Oracion' (Call to Prayer) every day so we know exactly what is going on in Evangelism in Depth all over the country. I will never forget May 7, National Visitation Day for Evangelism in Depth. We went out to visit. I went with fear. I didn't know what they would say. Tears of joy ran down my face that day because eight persons of those that I visited gave their hearts to the Lord. Now we have new courage."

One of Bolivia's co-presidents in 1965 was President Ovando Candia, who said the following during a luncheon at the close of Evangelism in Depth in Bolivia:

"Our most sincere appreciation for the privilege you give us of sharing the bread and salt of evangelical hospitality with you . . . I would also like to recognize the immense labor of the evangelical church in Bolivia. It has opened the doors of culture to the humble ones of my people, it has given them possibilities of battling sickness, it has enabled them for the struggle of life. For this reason, in the name of the supreme government, in the name of the Bolivian people, I cannot do other than express my most sincere appreciation to those who contribute to the individual and collective aggrandizement of my fatherland.

"I sincerely believe, gentlemen, that your evangelical mission, the mission of taking the word of God to all the inhabitants of the world, is the mission of privileged men; you may be proud of that. You not only contribute to the improvement of the material life of the inhabitants, in this case of Bolivia; you also are the engineers of their souls, because matter and soul together constitute the essence of man who is made in the image of God. Thank you very much."

From Venezuela:

Eleazar Inciarte V., from Maracaibo, Venezuela, was active in Evangelism in Depth in that country in 1964; now a leader with a music ministry, he was interviewed in 1987:
"I have continued with the idea of Evangelism in Depth by means of the musical ministry and the idea of united choirs in our cities. Also in Colombia they have continued with concerts by united choirs.

"Christian unity also has remained as a seed in Venezuela, so that when they are going to have a campaign, it is easier to get unity. We've had the first and second Venezuelan Evangelical Congresses that included evangelization and where those of us who had worked in Evangelism in Depth were experts in many of the fields that were discussed in the two congresses. For me, they were a continuation of Evangelism in Depth.

"Two national campaigns were held in Caracas at the end, on the same style as 23 years ago in Evangelism in Depth. I sincerely believe that when we had Evangelism in Depth there were only about 20,000 evangelicals in Venezuela and today there are around 1,700,000. The number has multiplied at least 100 times over.

"I believe that EID was a model of how to evangelize and it was a school for the churches which participated. Interestingly, the churches or denominations that did not take part in EID were not willing to cooperate for the two Evangelical Congresses in 1979 and 1984 either.

"Many of the converts of Evangelism in Depth are permanent. I have noted that in the united choirs we have organized, many in the rehearsals testified that they were products of Evangelism in Depth, particularly by means of the music and the first united national choir in the history of Venezuela. We will never forget the experience of having led so many to the feet of Jesus Christ; this is the truth."

The Rev. German Nunez, Baptist pastor in Caracas, Venezuela, was interviewed in 1986:
"What we learned in Evangelism in Depth continues, but it comes in spurts; God has sent several movements in the history of the evangelical work in our country and each movement has been used by God to add one more step.

"Evangelism in Depth, for one thing, brought us much instruction for evangelism and for another, an inspiration that has not left us. Furthermore it represents a great good for the evangelical people, for the various churches in the sense of being more united. We united and this brought salvation to many souls that have continued faithful, and also the consecration of many believers, the call of men to the Lord's service and it has continued to grow, and then we have had other events such as the First Evangelical Congress in Venezuela which continued this ascending march of the evangelical work in my country.''

From Mexico:

Presbyter Lenin Izquierdo, vice president of the Gulf Presbytery of the National Presbyterian Church in Mexico from 1983 to 1984, and president of the Presbytery from 1984 to 1985:
"As pastors, one of the results of Total Mobilization has been more backing from the people who have been trained. They are cooperating a lot. Many people are cooperating on the level of the entire field; there are 150 helpers prepared in the training courses. In 1983 the only helpers we had were the seven elders.

"We have founded four new congregations and four new missions. In our field probably 30 per cent of the people are new converts. In 1983 we had between 60 and 70 baptisms, and in 1984 we baptized 88; before 1983 we would baptize five on the average.

"There is now more confidence, more freedom in relationships between the elders and the people. Precisely the growth of the lay people has made the elders open up more.

"All the missions now have church buildings that didn't exist two years ago.

"I would recommend Total Mobilization to other places for three reasons: For the opportunity of training all the people; because it does not use rigid methods but with some orientation the people use their own methods; because the greater part of the members feel motivated to participate in evangelism. They feel that evangelism is within their reach; before, they thought they couldn't do it, but now it is different.

"From March 12 to 15 we had some 600 campaigns, and we had at least 12,000 people converted through them.''

Jonas Diaz de Dios, evangelism commission of the Christian Endeavor Union, Gulf Presbytery of National Presbyterian Church, 1985:
"For me more than anything Total Mobilization has been of great benefit, not only for those of us who already believe in Jesus, but also for those who have been converted through the movement. In Sinai they had several campaigns with much success and we have all the statistics; the majority of those converted are still in the church . . . .

"In 1985, 450 people were converted. There is a new positive attitude; for example, a new field was opened in Monte Moriah initiated by the Christian Endeavor, while they were involved in Total Mobilization.

"Total Mobilization has helped me a great deal. It has served as inspiration, I have learned to mobilize, and that's what it's all about. The believers thought that evangelism was the job of the pastor or full-time worker; they weren't accustomed to doing it and in truth they were ashamed to evangelize, but no longer. Many are now involved in doing the visitation; it's no longer something special but something common."

Presbyter Carmen Santana, pastor and member of the Christian Education Department, Gulf Presbytery, National Presbyterian Church, 1985:
    "We are talking of some 20,000 new people converted in these campaigns. The Latin America Mission of Mexico has definitely considered the local leadership in advising this movement. Previously someone would come to train, teach, and then leave; the only thing that remained was their image. But now a great deal has remained: strong leadership and a strong desire for improvement.

    "For example, in the training seminars from October 22 to November 2, 100 people were trained to preach in Arenal, 100 in Platano y Cacao; 100 in Pejelagartero; and 250 in Comalcalco. Other courses on how to preach well were given in Comalcalco, Villahermosa, Cardenas, and Arenal and we estimate that 100 attended in each place.

    "Before this movement the work was carried out but not with much energy or dedication. It was done by just a few people; the majority did nothing.

    "Evangelism in Depth is disquieting, it awakens interest, it emphasizes the concepts in the yellow book *(How to Succeed in Evangelism in Depth).* It can be said that the majority was mobilized; not all, because that can never be achieved, but the majority is definitely interested . . . .

    "For example, on April 4 the Philadelphia church evangelized its entire field.

    "The growth of the congregation is another concept that is always present and this can be proved. We have grown, the number of believers has augmented, and these believers are true ones that can be counted.

    "Yes, an interest in going on has been awakened, an interest in evangelism. Also, Evangelism in Depth has the purpose of discovering new leaders and this can also be proved, since many people that were inactive now have something to do. I learned that an abundant harvest always requires abundant sowing. The fact that a consecrated minority can make an impact on an entire nation has made an impression on me; I emphasized this in all my field. For example, since April 4 visitation has gone on continuously. All the people got moving and got organized. And we have about 50 prayer cells in action. In 1984, 100 people were baptized in my field and another 150 were converted."

Jose Maria Priego, state coordinator of Evangelism in Depth, Gulf Presbytery, National Presbyterian Church, 1985:
    "The results that we have been able to prove in the places where we have had activities, are very satisfactory. For example, we have churches

that doubled their number of members following the Day of Impact with visitation. They are amazed to see the quantity of new converts in their churches.

"One small mission which pertains to the number 9 region, of the Bethel church, is called La Florida mission. Although there were only 40 believers, they went out to visit on the Day of Impact and reached 60 homes. That same day they held an evangelistic meeting and had 35 new converts, and seeing the results, they went on for a second and third day, and now they have 68 new converts and the mission has more than 100 members.

"We have had between 3,900 and 4,000 prayer cells registered in Total Mobilization; data is lacking from some of the regions where they reached very large numbers. I think there are more than 10,000 prayer cells in all."

Roberto Bolon, Presbyterian layman from Jonuta, Tabasco, Mexico, 1983:
"In 20 days we were all mobilized because we were really interested and now we feel joy and happiness. Everyone in the choir is new. We have visited from Jonuta on down, that is, Jonuta, Pino Suarez, Monte do los Olivos, Jesus de Nazaret, and Bethel.

"When I have to go out on the work of Total Mobilization I close my store, and many times when I return I sell a double amount."

Presbyter Cesar Montiel, Presbyterian pastor, Tabasco, Mexico, 1983:
"Sixty people went out to visit. Total Mobilization is something extraordinary . . . there are more people now who wish to cooperate. We have 30 per cent more people than in 1982; before we would receive 10 or 15 new people a year but now in 1983 we received 33 new members. We have two new missions.

"It is a movement with new techniques that facilitate not only the mobilization of the church but also a more effective outreach to the unconverted and a more realistic way of using the human resources which a church might have, thus making possible the fulfillment of the mission of the church in a more effective way. This does facilitate the mobilization and growth of the church."

Architect Sergio Cantu, pastor of the God is Love Presbyterian Church, Satelite City, Mexico, 1988:
"Three months after the Evangelism in Depth seminar, I can say the course is excellent, of great usefulness, very dynamic, for the churches that are bogged down in a rut . . . we have had growth; it's been necessary to use more chairs each Sunday and the Bible studies have grown with the idea of developing more missions. The people show great interest, there are many new people, we can't handle it all.

"To be congruent with Christ's commandment the problem is not confessing the truth but communicating it."

The Rev. Regino Palazuelos, national coordinator of Evangelism in Depth in Mexico, 1970-72, interviewed in 1988:
"Evangelism in Depth in Mexico brought several benefits, but two are outstanding. First, openness toward the fellowship of the different denominations. Before 1970, which was when we celebrated Evangelism in Depth, the denominational leaders were a bit separate. Not that we did not have relationships, but we looked at one another at a bit of a distance. To be able to fellowship together is a great benefit that EID brought us, and today after 18 years I see . . . the denominational leaders live together more closely.

"The second benefit is that on that occasion we knew little regarding the philosophies of evangelization, above all with regard to the mobilization of our membership, and of the leadership within the church. At that time this principle of lay leadership was not very well developed. EID provided us with a very good formation.

"Officially we had about 6,900 churches registered at that time, but more than 9,000 participated although they were not all officially registered. Thousands of people were trained. The country is so large that we divided it by regions; we had more than 37 regions.

"The parades: I remember I attended several that were very notable for me. From Mazatlan I have photos; the one we had here in Mexico City was very impressive as well, on March 21, with more than 50,000 people; and another large parade was celebrated in the state of Nuevo Leon.

"Yes, the denominations continue practicing the principles of Evangelism in Depth. Never before — and I am sure of what I am saying — had we experienced such a great awakening for the evangelization of our country as during those days. I consider that the seed that was sown in Evangelism in Depth has sprouted and grown to maturity.

"In the Church of God we learned this philosophy of work and we are practicing it and I understand that the Assemblies of God were also very much benefitted by this work. I know some other denominations and independent churches that are carrying out total mobilization. It not only produces immediate fruit, but also fruit over the long term."

Professor Samuel Noguera, pastor of Jerusalem Missionary Church, Tepeapulco, Hidalgo, Mexico, 1986:
"Personally I believe that Evangelism in Depth was an absolute blessing in different areas of Christian development. First in the spiritual area, the life of prayer and mobilization was fomented in some brethren who had been inactive for several years. On the other hand we see growth in the number of people attending church services and Sunday School.

"Of course there were abundant finances. The missions were fortified and the number of people in attendance grew.

"My opinion is that it was a very blessed program. At this point we have 24 new missions as a result of Evangelism in Depth, plus ten new missions in Loma Bonita and seven new missions of the Bethany church. The young people are evangelizing on the street every Saturday and there are prayer meetings every Saturday, and they are also doing their own Bible studies. Many families now practice family worship."

The Rev. Joas Gomez, pastor Mount Sinai Methodist Church, Satelite City, Mexico, 1988:

"That Evangelism in Depth seminar brought very positive results in the enthusiasm of the brethren, their faith, their desire to testify for Jesus Christ and share with others the salvation that they have found, the joy, the peace, and this has produced benefits for all the congregation . . . .

"I recommend it fully for any place where it can be carried out. Positively it is a blessing for every congregation or for all the Christian public in order to learn how to communicate the Gospel to the lost and to those who are still in darkness.

"I recommend this seminar first because it brings a revival for the people who participate in it, and secondly because this revival has repercussions in all the church, and all the church begins to work and give testimony and preach the Gospel to every creature. The teachings are completely biblical, completely orthodox from the point of view of the Gospel and because of that I recommend it fully."

The Rev. Guillermo Haro Valencia, pastor Mount Hermon Church of the Mission of the Seventy, Mexico City, 1988:

"When we had the Evangelism in Depth seminar January 29 to 31, we had 344 people registered in our church including children. Today, May 19, we have more than 720 people registered including children. We have grown particularly during the past two months.

"The teaching that every person can evangelize has remained in the church. In this case the Christians had tried for years to witness to their neighbors but this fact of feeling themselves evangelizers was used by God to give them power so that now those neighbors are in the church. The new people are really integrated into the church . . . .

"At present we no longer fit in the church building and we are preparing a tent. Since three weeks ago we have been preparing the people to make the move, since the test will have space for more than 2,000 people and they are going to feel lost in such a big place, but we think the Christians will feel even more motivated to witness. The growth is going to continue because the congregation is very motivated. The tent will be attractive not only for the church people but for outsiders.

"Since February, when I preach on Sundays I include music with the preaching.

"My first reason for recommending Evangelism in Depth, is that a growing church is a church which is pleasing to God. Furthermore, we teach people. Those who attend do not feel like Christians in just a general sense but they realize they are active members of the Lord Jesus Christ, not just active members of the church, and all this growth implies blessing because we have experienced it. Thirdly, because I learned something from Evangelism in Depth's little yellow book, that it is a romance to live with EID. The church is growing every day."

The Rev. Filiberto Pacheco, founder and director, Mission of the Seventy, Mexico, 1988:
"Since I had the opportunity and the blessing of accompanying Juan Isais to Brazil, where I listened to the testimonies of every one of the people who were interviewed regarding their opinion of Evangelism in Depth, I must say that I received it like a loving embrace from God, because when the Mission of the Seventy was born I always desired growth and I continue to desire it . . . .

"In addition to the fact that the people are getting mobilized, they are entering into their first love, something that motivates them to see people saved and this is what is happening."

Materials Currently Available on First Love Renewals

The Songs of First Love Renewal: sheet music of some of the popular choruses used in seminars. $2.00 postpaid

The Songs of First Love Renewal: Cassette tape of popular choruses used in seminars and designed with a performance side for use in public worship. Words included on jacket. $5.00 plus shipping

First Love Renewal Syllabus; Includes lessons with answer sheets, manual, music resources, in binder. $15.00 plus shipping

The Other Evangelism: by Juan M. Isais. The principles and philosophy of Evangelism in Depth as shared by one of its pioneers.
$5.00 plus shipping

For futher information and materials on
First Love Renewal, write:

Brethren Evangelistic Ministries
P.O. Box 333
Winona Lake, Indiana 46590